MW00564366

Global Political Thinkers

Series Editors
Harmut Behr
School of Geography Politics & Sociology
Newcastle University
Newcastle, UK

Felix Rösch
School of Humanities
Coventry University
Coventry, UK

This Palgrave Pivot series presents ground-breaking, critical perspectives on political theory: titles published in this series present influential political thinkers on a global scale from around the world, with interpretations based on their original languages, providing synoptic views on their works, and written by internationally leading scholars. Individual interpretations emphasize the language and cultural context of political thinkers and of political theory as primary media through which political thoughts and concepts originate and generate. The series invites proposals for new Palgrave Pivot projects by and on authors from all traditions, areas, and cultural contexts. Individual books should be between 25,000 and 50,000 words long according to the Palgrave Pivot format. For more details about Palgrave Pivot, an innovative new publishing format from Palgrave Macmillan, please visit www.palgrave.com/pivot. Emphases shall be on political thinkers who are important for our understanding of: - the relation between individual and society and conceptualizations of both; - forms of participation and decision-making; - conceptualizations of political deliberation and discourse; - constructions of identity; - conceptualizations of the 'human condition' of politics; - ontologies and epistemologies of the political/of politics; - conceptualizations of social and political change and/or tradition; and - conceptualizations of political order, their rise and fall

More information about this series at
http://www.palgrave.com/gp/series/15014

Lisandro E. Claudio

Jose Rizal

Liberalism and the Paradox of Coloniality

Lisandro E. Claudio
De La Salle University
Manila, Philippines

Global Political Thinkers
ISBN 978-3-030-01315-8   ISBN 978-3-030-01316-5   (eBook)
https://doi.org/10.1007/978-3-030-01316-5

Library of Congress Control Number: 2018958886

© The Editor(s) (if applicable) and The Author(s) 2019
This work is subject to copyright. All rights are solely and exclusively licensed by the Publisher, whether the whole or part of the material is concerned, specifically the rights of translation, reprinting, reuse of illustrations, recitation, broadcasting, reproduction on microfilms or in any other physical way, and transmission or information storage and retrieval, electronic adaptation, computer software, or by similar or dissimilar methodology now known or hereafter developed.
The use of general descriptive names, registered names, trademarks, service marks, etc. in this publication does not imply, even in the absence of a specific statement, that such names are exempt from the relevant protective laws and regulations and therefore free for general use. The publisher, the authors and the editors are safe to assume that the advice and information in this book are believed to be true and accurate at the date of publication. Neither the publisher nor the authors or the editors give a warranty, express or implied, with respect to the material contained herein or for any errors or omissions that may have been made. The publisher remains neutral with regard to jurisdictional claims in published maps and institutional affiliations.

Cover pattern © Melisa Hasan

This Palgrave Macmillan imprint is published by the registered company Springer Nature Switzerland AG
The registered company address is: Gewerbestrasse 11, 6330 Cham, Switzerland

For Christine

PROLOGUE

Contemporary liberalism is synonymous with moderation. It is a philosophy of mainstream governance and compromise, often challenged by more radical beliefs from populists, socialists, neo-fascists—agitators from all sides of the political spectrum. But this same philosophy was the key radical idea of the nineteenth century, a century birthed in revolution—a time when memories of the French and American revolutions served as calls to liberty across continents and oceans.

To conjure the revolutionary élan of the period, we may visit the cradles of these calls to liberty, places like the United States and France. But doing so would not only be a tired project but also fail to grasp the extent of liberalism's appeal. Liberalism spread much farther than Eurocentric versions of its history assume, and the goal of this work is to find liberalism in an unlikely place. Recent work has traced the movement of liberal thought to various places in the Caribbean (Polasky 2015). But how about Asia?

The polymath intellectual Jose Rizal was a novelist, poet, physician, naturalist, essayist, artist, linguist, and historian. His writings inspired the anti-Spanish Philippine Revolution of 1896—the first anti-colonial revolution in Asia. For his nationalism, he is revered as his country's national hero, appearing on the country's money, its monuments, its street signs, its schools. The law requires all Filipino students to read his novels. And debates about the minutiae of his life make nationalist historians apoplectic. Whether or not he retracted his anti-Catholic writings before death, whether or not he supported the revolution—these questions remain central to how historians and citizens of the Philippines view their nation.

Some scholars—the historian of nationalism Benedict Anderson to name the most prominent—have championed Rizal's relevance to global political thought, and the recent publication of Rizal's novels as part of the Penguin Classics series has broadened his English-speaking audience. Slowly, Rizal is being ensconced in the world republic of letters.

Within the "Malay" world of Indonesia and Malaysia, Rizal commands a modest following for being a "pride of the Malayan race" (he was a Chinese mestizo).[1] Such a reading of Rizal has expanded his relevance outside the Philippines, but can remain tied to racialist conceptions of politics that, at least in Malaysia, dovetail with Malay state formation.[2] In any case, Filipinos themselves rarely think in terms of racial categories like Malay, even though Rizal was, at times, prone to racialist, even racist, conceptions of nationalism.

Despite the growth of Rizal scholarship, his influence has by and large been limited to his country, especially in the area of political philosophy. This limited influence is hardly surprising for someone who, by the 1890s, had decided to jettison European readers, seeking to speak directly to his *patria*. Audience mattered to Rizal. His novels—so specific in their setting, lexicon, humor, and political concerns—must be read as Filipino texts. They remain vivid introductions to life in late nineteenth-century Philippines, with Rizal serving as a satirical tour guide of a new nation teeming with revolutionary energy. Through his books, one learns about the hypocrisy of the friar orders, the fecklessness of reforms, and the resentment of a people ready to revolt. These novels also conjure the Philippines as definite place—with its distinct cultural practices, cuisine, patois—albeit centered on Manila and the Tagalog-speaking provinces. How do we draw universal lessons from a man focused on local issues?

Rizal had specific concerns, and his commentary was drawn from a unique milieu: the earliest pro-independence nationalist movement in Asia that was also the last pro-independence nationalist movement within the Spanish empire. It is tempting to view Rizal and his country as exceptional: neither Asian nor Latin American. And nationalist Filipinos may even

---

[1] Malaysia's Anwar Ibrahim, both as a member of the administration UMNO Party and as an opposition leader, has spoken fondly of Rizal as a Malay leader.

[2] This racialist thinking is partly reflected in the thought of Indonesian nationalist Tan Malaka who saw Rizal as part of a "Greater Indonesia" torn asunder by colonialism (Guillermo 2017). But Tan Malaka's vision of Rizal, unlike those of the Malay nationalists in Malaysia, places more emphasis on anti-colonial solidarity.

entertain some form of pride in the unique nature of the life and times of their national hero. Yet specific need not mean parochial. Rizal was an Enlightenment figure, and while he commented almost exclusively on the events in his country, his ideas drew from a wellspring of transnational political thought.

Rizal's ideas were anchored on the traditions of Republican Spain, the place where the current usage of the term "liberalism" was born. The Spain of the nineteenth century was a center for liberal internationalism, where secret organizations, Masonic lodges, and various conspiracies theorized what were then subversive ideas about Enlightenment. Spanish liberals were inspired by the French Revolution, but they also developed their own liberal heritage.

Rizal's writings, primarily his novels, drew from the world of French Enlightenment: from Voltaire, Dumas, and Hugo.[3] And his conception of rights was anchored on the major declarations of the time, from the French Declaration of the Rights of Man (a document he translated from French into Tagalog), the American Declaration of independence, to Spain's liberal Cadiz Constitution. But he was no mere copycat. Despite acknowledging the derivative quality in some of his writings, Rizal was confident that his context gave him a unique voice. Rizal knew that his works would not share the aplomb of authors like Hugo, and he felt a nagging sense that his work lacked the artistic merit of those penned by European masters. His insecurities notwithstanding, he knew that his books were special because they rehearsed the themes of liberty and freedom in a colonial context.

My goal in these pages is to view liberalism obliquely, from a vista rarely explored. What would liberalism look like when seen through the eyes of liberals in the colony? Rizal is one of colonial/postcolonial liberalism's earliest and most prescient thinkers. He may also well be Asia's pioneering liberal. Prior to Sun Yat-Sen or Nehru, Rizal was already thinking about what freedom, liberty, and rights meant in colonial contexts. In Southeast Asia, Rizal would not have an equivalent until the 1930s. Perhaps his closest analogue is the Vietnamese novelist and journalist Vũ Trọng Phụng, who melded the liberal and republican ideals of the French third republic with anti-colonialism (Zinoman 2014). Like Rizal, Vũ Trọng Phụng has

---

[3] Rizal was likewise inspired by European (particularly German) ethnology, anthropology, historiography, and linguistics. His ideas on these matters have been discussed in other work (see Thomas 2012; Ocampo 2013, 75–117; Mojares 2013, 126–137; Aguilar 2005).

been belatedly recognized as an exemplary realist novelist, whose use of satire exposed the contradictions of colonial rule.

The tragedy is that many authors and readers neglect Rizal's liberalism, perhaps because postcolonial thinkers find it difficult to view liberalism alongside anti-colonialism. Postcolonial theory, as Vivek Chibber (2014, 618) has argued, exhibits a "boilerplate skepticism" against any forms of "Western" Enlightenment. Hence many recent works have identified the liberal cause with that of imperialism. In the Philippines, which has its own historiographical tradition that trades on the demonization of anything "Western,"[4] Rizal is barely discussed as a liberal. For how could the national hero of an Asian country be an advocate of an idea as foreign as liberalism?

Although some writers from the Maoist Communist Party of the Philippines write of Rizal as liberal, they do so to point out his incomplete political development—his lack of a systematic class-based vision. For Communist Party of the Philippines founder, Jose Maria Sison (1966), for example, "the anticolonial and anticlerical writings of Rizal" stemmed from a "now outmoded liberal cast," despite its influence during his time.

We cannot deny the provenance of liberalism; it was born in Europe in an era of pan-Atlanticism. And the earliest liberal revolutions occurred in places like England, the United States, and France—polities that officially remain committed to liberal democratic governance. And we also cannot deny that many imperial crusades, aimed at spreading "civilization," drew from liberal ideas about linear progress. Yet because liberalism is a philosophy of openness and toleration, it is also the philosophy with the most myriad vectors: a philosophy of openness is likewise open to interpretation. The liberalism of Spain, and certainly that of France or America, would have been different from the liberalism of the Philippines. Rizal was aware of these differences, even as he acknowledged the common Enlightenment heritage of all liberalisms.

How was liberalism interpreted in colonial contexts? The answer is not obvious since liberal philosophy resonates with people advocating different causes. There were, indeed, Western, liberal colonizers who saw no contradiction between their liberal beliefs and imperialism (Mehta 1999). In fact, some of them believed that liberal rights could only be spread to non-Western societies through colonialism. On the other hand, there were liberals who saw colonialism as a contradiction of liberal values.

---

[4] See Claudio 2017, 13–17, for a discussion of this movement, which I call the "Diliman Consensus." For an earlier take on the same phenomenon, see Claudio 2013.

I hope to show that the more ethical liberalism was articulated not by those who advocated imperialism, but by those who rebelled against it, by people like Rizal and his cohort of nationalist intellectuals, the so-called Filipino "ilustrados" of the late nineteenth century. Through Rizal, I seek to expand my analysis of postcolonial liberalism (see Claudio 2017), and to argue for this liberalism's relevance in contemporary postcolonies, or what scholars sometimes refer to as "the Global South." If my earlier work traced the role of liberalism in state formation in the early twentieth-century Philippines, this work looks at liberalism's contribution to Filipino national imagination in the nineteenth. Both works contend that liberals in the colony understand something about liberty that liberals in empire do not. The experience of colonial oppression affords them special insight into the nature of freedom and rights. In this book, I argue that liberty is more precarious in colonies, and colonial liberals know that freedoms and rights have to be earned through suffering and pain.

Like my previous work, I wish to define liberalism through intellectual biography as opposed to didactic conceptual mapping. Therefore, I will only define liberalism in the broadest terms. I agree with Alan Ryan (2012, 28) who notes that liberalism, in all its guises, has been "a perennial protest against absolute forms of absolute authority." But unlike anarchism, liberals have sought to find order in freedom. Walter Russel Mead (2013) distills liberal thought as such: "Even though humanity is imperfect and flawed, that does not mean we cannot have constitutional, political, and social arrangements that, given the limits on man's nature, can at least provide a society where the individual is as unconstrained as possible."

In other words, there are institutional arrangements that promote individual rights and freedoms. And it is the task of the liberal to scrutinize and test these various arrangements. The institution of colonialism was, of course, a failure in this regard. In the twentieth century, George Orwell would even view it as a form of totalitarianism, akin to the dictatorships of the Nazis and the Soviet Communists. Yet we need not rely on European thinkers for anti-authoritarian/totalitarian attacks on colonialism.

Rizal is the ideal thinker for our purposes, not only because of his prominence, but because he theorized liberty more than any of his contemporaries. Liberalism was the overarching lens through which Rizal viewed politics. And, as we shall see, it was Rizal's liberalism that led him to his pro-independence position. If he was a subversive in nineteenth-century Philippines, it was because he was a staunch liberal in a reactionary colony.

Rizal's thinking was defined by liberalism. Still, I recognize that the Rizal I will represent in these pages is also specific to my own concerns and the concerns of the world today. I agree with the most celebrated Rizal scholar, Ambeth Ocampo (2013, 6), who argues that "Rizal was and is a different man to different people in different times." His biography, his ideas, and his legacy have served various political and ideological purposes, not only because interpretations vary, but also because Rizal was a complex thinker who addressed multiple concerns using multiple lenses. To focus on his liberalism may leave out or underemphasize other facets of his philosophy. Any historian must prioritize, and I have prioritized Rizal's liberalism, for both empirical and political reasons.

If I seek to write into historiography a liberal Rizal, it is partly because a liberal Rizal is necessary at a time of illiberalism. As I write this, multiple countries are sliding into illiberal democracy, where populist politicians are elected and celebrated not in spite of, but because they challenge norms such as human rights and rule of law. In these states, taboos about acceptable political behavior and speech are broken every day, so that ideas once considered immoral are now normal. In 2016, Rizal's own country elected a mass murderer, who sees human rights as "liberal" inventions of the West. "Catholic" Filipinos who once valued the sanctity of life then endorsed a war on drugs that resulted in thousands of state-sanctioned executions. The Philippines is proof of how quickly voters dispense with what were once sacrosanct values in favor of appeals to base instincts. From the liberal nationalism of Jose Rizal, the country degenerated into the authoritarian barbarism of President Rodrigo Duterte. In writing about Rizal, I seek to remind Rizal's compatriots that liberalism and human rights are not foreign impositions; they were integral facets of our national imagination.

The reader who hates being preached at, however, has little to fear, as this book is not a political pamphlet. Despite the political crisis that subtends its writing, it is primarily introduction to readers who are encountering Rizal for the first time. And despite my own desire to speak to Filipinos at a critical juncture, this book's main audience is the non-Filipino reader, who did not grow up learning about Rizal in school.

This book is not concerned with the many biographical debates that Filipino Rizalists have engaged in over the years (e.g. whether or not Rizal died a Catholic, or whether or not he lent his support to the Philippine Revolution of 1896 that overthrew Spain). Rather, my goal is to outline

Rizal's thoughts on principles such as liberty and freedom in colonial contexts, and to do so for the broadest audience possible. I also seek to introduce readers to Rizal's most important works. My sources will therefore be the most easily accessible translations of Rizal's writings, except in those cases where a closer reading of the original Spanish proves necessary. The core texts are three: the collection of Rizal's writings and correspondences published by the National Historical Commission of the Philippines and his two novels, *Noli Me Tangere* (Touch Me Not) and *El Filibusterismo* (Subversion) which, like most Filipinos, I refer to as "The *Noli*" and "The *Fili*" respectively. In discussions of the novels, I will quote from the widely available Penguin translations by Harold Augenbaum. Since I refer to these works multiple times, I have used a shorthand citation method for them, which I explain in the bibliography. For greater simplicity and to reflect linguistic practice in contemporary Philippines, I have also Filipinized Spanish-derived words by removing accents, except in cases of direct quotation.

Apart from contributing to global political theory, a secondary goal is to introduce non-Filipino readers to the best of Rizal scholarship written mostly, though not exclusively, by Filipinos published in the Philippines. I have consciously made an attempt to consult and cite liberally from these works, because they have been the most consistent with the spirit of Rizal's own writing—writing that carries global resonance, ironically, because they are anchored on local realities.

This short book cannot be anything but an introduction. Yet it hopes to do a bit more. Beyond getting to know Rizal, my hope is that the reader and future writers start to think about the horizons and limits of liberalism and its role in colonial/postcolonial contexts. The first chapter situates Rizal life and works in the context of late nineteenth-century Philippines, a period of economic growth and political awakening. Chapter 2 mines Rizal's political writings and correspondences to sketch his overarching vision of liberty in the colony. His central vision, I contend, is that liberty becomes purified through the pain and suffering of colonial peoples. Chapters 3 and 4 provide readers with introductions to Rizal's novels, using Rizal's liberalism as a philosophical backdrop.

The focus on the novels is deliberate. Although there is much to be said about Rizal's verse, his philological work, his historiographic work, and even his research in the natural sciences, Rizal will be remembered as a novelist. In any case, he was a first-class fictionist, and a second-rate historian, too prone to letting propagandistic goals distort historical fact.

Moreover, I am certain that most non-Filipino readers are more interested in literature than anthropological arcana.

I have, unsurprisingly, incurred a number of debts prior to and while working on this book. I extend my deepest appreciation to Kyoto University's Caroline S. Hau, who convinced me to tackle what I had previously thought of as a trite topic. This is not the first time Carol has pushed me outside my comfort zone, and probably won't be the last. Apart from Carol, much of my thinking on Rizal has been shaped by the immense work of two great Filipino historians, Resil Mojares and Ambeth Ocampo. Ambeth, Carol, and Jojo Abinales also read this manuscript and provided valuable feedback.

Felix Rösch and Hartmut Behr, the editors of Palgrave Pivot's Global Political Thinkers series, believed Rizal to be important to global political thought, and entrusted me with making the case for him. Megan Thomas trusted me enough to endorse me to Felix and Hartmut.

I worked on this manuscript during my first year at De La Salle University, and benefited greatly from the support of La Salle's College of Liberal Arts and University Research Coordination Office. My thanks to Dean Jaz Llana, Research Coordinator Feorillo Demeterio, former Dean July Teehankee, Rene Escalante, Ronnie Holmes, Fernie Santiago, Xiao Chua, Jeremy de Chavez, Ricky San Jose, Beth Gabiosa, Babyln Batlanggao, Chris Collantes, JJ Joaquin, Kat Gutierrez, Ron Vilog, Bubbles Asor, Mikee Inton, Cleo Calimbahin, Che Soriano, Phil Binondo, Nelson Tantoco, and Bro. Armin Luistro, FSC.

I remain indebted to my alma mater, Ateneo de Manila, and to my friends and colleagues there, in particular Filomeno Aguilar, Jayeel Cornelio, Jowel Canuday, Melay Abao, Melissa Lao, and Niño Leviste.

Outside the Philippines, I thank Nicole Curato, Kate McGregor, Jafar Suryomenggolo, Nicole CuUnjieng-Aboitiz, Mario Lopez, Sheila Coronel, Julius Bautista, Mike Montesano, Sharmila Parmanand, Jon Ong, Jason Cabañes, and Tomas Larsson. I thank Tomas and Jayeel in particular for making me part of a grant that aided with research. This research was aided by the European Union's Horizon 2020 research and innovation program under grant agreement N°770562.

Marriage has given me a new family: Alex, Nancy, Jack, Mark, and Kate Herrin. Then there is my old family: my parents, Rafael and Sylvia, and my brothers Bas and Redd. My final thanks is for my wife, Christine Herrin, to whom this work is dedicated.

BIBLIOGRAPHY

Aguilar, Filomeno V. 2005. Tracing Origins: Ilustrado Nationalism and the Racial Science of Migration Waves. *The Journal of Asian Studies* 64 (03): 605–637.

Chibber, Vivek. 2014. Making Sense of Postcolonial Theory: A Response to Gayatri Chakravorty Spivak. *Cambridge Review of International Affairs* 27 (3): 617–624.

Claudio, Lisandro E. 2013. Postcolonial Fissures and the Contingent Nation An Antinationalist Critique of Philippine Historiography. *Philippine Studies: Historical and Ethnographic Viewpoints* 61 (1): 45–75.

———. 2017. *Liberalism and the Postcolony: Thinking the State in 20th-Century Philippines*. Singapore: NUS Press.

Guillermo, Ramon. 2017. Andres Bonifacio: Proletarian Hero of the Philippines and Indonesia. *Inter-Asia Cultural Studies* 18 (3): 338–346.

Mead, Walter Russell. 2013. A Historical Look at American Liberalism. Interview by Charles R. Kesler. Youtube Video, September 12. https://www.youtube.com/watch?v=pRCTg5OWlZs

Mehta, Uday Singh. 1999. *Liberalism and Empire*. Chicago and London: University of Chicago Press.

Mojares, Resil B. 2013. *Isabelo's Archive*. Manila: Anvil Publishing Inc.

Ocampo, Ambeth R. 2013. *Meaning and History: The Rizal Lectures*. Revised ed. Pasig City: Anvil Publishing Inc.

Polasky, Janet. 2015. *Revolutions Without Borders: The Call to Liberty in the Atlantic World*. New Haven: Yale University Press.

Ryan, Alan. 2012. *The Making of Modern Liberalism*. Princeton/Oxford: Princeton University Press.

Sison, Jose Maria. 1966. Rizal the Social Critic, December 29. https://josemaria-sison.org/rizal-the-social-critic/

Thomas, Megan C. 2012. *Orientalists, Propagandists, and Ilustrados: Filipino Scholarship and the End of Spanish Colonialism*. Minneapolis/London: University of Minnesota Press

Zinoman, Peter. 2013. *Vietnamese Colonial Republican: The Political Vision of Vũ Trọng Phụng*. Berkeley: University of California Press.

CONTENTS

1   Creolism and the Liberal Nineteenth Century   1

2   Pain and the Purification of Liberty   21

3   *Noli me Tangere* and the Failure of Transplanted Liberalism   37

4   The Solution of the Enigma in *El Filibusterismo*   55

5   Conclusion: Resurrecting Plants   71

Shorthand Citations for Rizal's Works   79

Bibliography   81

Index   85

CHAPTER 1

Creolism and the Liberal Nineteenth Century

Abstract This chapter situates the life of Jose Rizal. First, it examines the origins of Philippine liberalism in the creole intellectuals of the late eighteenth century/early nineteenth century. It explains how these creoles, inspired by the French Revolution and other liberal movements in Europe, articulated the broad contours of the propaganda movement that Rizal would lead in the nineteenth century. Second, it provides an overview of the political and economic changes in the Philippines during the late nineteenth century. It was a period of economic growth and political stagnation, creating a revolutionary atmosphere that would form not only the ideas of Rizal but also the Philippine Revolution of 1896. It ends with a brief biography of Rizal.

Keywords Creoles • Nationalism • Ilustrados • Rizal • Filipino liberals

Although this book is about a global idea, we must begin our story locally. For the context in which Rizal wrote was specific, and some might even say anomalous. It is now routine for historians of the Philippines to claim that Rizal's writings inspired the nationalist revolution of the Kataastaasan, Kagalang-galang na Katipunan nang Manga Anak ng Bayan (The Supreme and Most Honorable Society of the Children of the Nation), the Katipunan, or the KKK for short. And recent historiography has shown

L. E. Claudio, *Jose Rizal*, Global Political Thinkers,
https://doi.org/10.1007/978-3-030-01316-5_1

that the Katipunan's revolution of 1896, which overthrew Spanish colonial rule, was Rizalian inasmuch as it espoused an anti-colonial, liberal agenda and not, as previously thought, a utopian and socialist/millenarian one (see Rafael 2015 for a summary of this new historiography).

The Philippine Revolution was the first anti-colonial revolution in Asia. But it was the last in the Spanish empire. It is this anomalous, revolutionary context that must frame our understanding of Rizal's work. For although Rizal was executed as the revolution was just starting, it was the broader radical ethos of the period that informed his thinking. The late nineteenth century was a time of liberal radicalism.

"Liberal radicalism" might sound like an anachronism today, since we equate liberalism with the status quo of the West. It is, notes Adam Kirsch (2016), "the air we [in the West] all breathe and the lens through which we see all political issues." But liberalism was the leading revolutionary ideology of the eighteenth and nineteenth centuries, and liberals were the main challengers of autocratic and religious governments the world over. Prior to the Bolshevik Revolution, it was the French and American revolutions that radicals looked toward for inspiration. As with the enslaved peoples of the Caribbean (Polasky 2015, 138), it was "rumors of freedom" that inspired liberal radicals in the Philippines. In the nineteenth century, news of events like the Paris Commune of 1871 and the Spanish Glorious Revolution 1868 would have made Filipino patriots believe in the continued vibrancy of liberal thought.

This chapter moves from broad to specific: from a history of Philippine liberalism prior to Rizal, to a history of the changes in the Philippines during the nineteenth century, to a short biography of Rizal himself. Beyond introducing Rizal, my aim is to show that liberalism was the key idea of early Filipino nationalist imagination and that this articulation of liberalism with nationalism was central to Rizal's political views.

LIBERALISM IN THE PHILIPPINES

The early history of nationalism is inevitably tied up with liberalism. To launch a liberal experiment in the New World, North Americans forged a civic-minded nationalism/patriotism to bind the various colonies. The different forces that sought to defend French revolutionary ideals—from the Girondins, to the Jacobins, to Napoleon—aroused support for their cause by claiming affinity to a fatherland. After the fall of Napoleon and the emergence of the Concert of Europe/Metternich system which sought to repress both nationalism and the ideas of the French Revolution, liberals and nationalists found common cause against a common reactionary foe. Much later, the architects of Italian unification, thinkers like Giuseppe Mazzini, saw the unified nation as the perfect symbol and vehicle for liberal thought.

In the Philippines, as in the Americas, the formation of a liberal-nationalist consciousness may be traced to the unique experiences of Europeans born in the colony—"creoles." Benedict Anderson's (1983, 47–66) work on nationalism shows that independence movements in Spanish and British America were both led by "creole pioneers," who were racially European, but developed greater attachments to their countries of birth. Since they could not obtain high-ranking positions in the metropole, their upward mobility circumscribed by the conditions of their birth, they began to imagine the colonies as separate fatherlands from the metropole.[1] Others, particularly the English-speaking creoles, decried unfair trade policies between North American colonies and Britain.

Although Anderson himself does not state it, these creoles were largely liberals. This point becomes evident when one examines the English-speaking creoles of North America, that is, the American founding fathers. In the figure of Thomas Jefferson, for example, we see an Englishman born in the colonies (creole), who develops a nationalist attachment to his place of birth, and writes the declaration of independence—one of the world's key liberal texts.

The origins of Philippine nationalism can likewise be traced to creole liberals. The emergence of "'modern' dissent" in the Philippines, explains Resil Mojares (2017, 27), occurred amid "the rise of liberalism in Spain and the Latin American revolutions of 1808–25," which "provided stimulus and space for political dissent in Manila and its environs, expressed in the activities of Creoles and secular priests who, invoking the entitlements of race and education, worked for greater autonomy within the colonial state." Though tame by Latin American standards, this early liberalism would paved the way for radical propagandists like Rizal.

---

[1] The category "creole," as we shall see, was more slippery in the Philippines. Unlike Latin America, there were fewer "pure" Spaniards in the Philippines, so creoles tended to marry more with the native "indio" population. Their offspring, however, continued to identify as "creoles" and were often associated with a form of liberal/nationalist politics known as "criollismo." Nevertheless, Filipino creoles, like their American counterparts, became key figures in their country's early nationalism.

The pre-eminent Filipino public intellectual of the twentieth century, Nick Joaquin (2005, 24) begins the story of Filipino nationalist propaganda with the early nineteenth-century creole Luis Rodriguez Varela. Varela was not just a liberal, who sought to bring the enlightenment of the French Revolution to the Philippines; he was also an early nationalist. He was the first writer to identify himself as a "Filipino," eventually taking on the moniker of "El Conde Filipino." Prior to the Conde, the term "Filipino" was simply an administrative designation for creoles from the Philippines, rarely used by these creoles themselves, who identified as Spaniards. It was through Varela that the term began to take on a political meaning.

In 1799, Varela published three books in defense of the liberalism and the Enlightenment. These early works were critical of the obscurantism of the friar orders—a theme central theme that would dominate liberal writing until Rizal's time. They were also pleas for a transplantation of Enlightenment principles into the colony. Varela admired the French Revolution, but grew wary of it when Napoleon captured the revolution and imposed his brother, Joseph Bonaparte, as king of Spain in 1808 (ibid., 29). For Varela, as with Rizal, liberalism was best expressed through an independent republic.

During this period, the fortunes of creoles in the Philippines were contingent on developments in Spain, and their confidence rose as political liberalism asserted itself at the center of Spanish politics. Unifying against the French, the Spanish set up the country's first sovereign assembly, the Cortes, in 1810. Though the Cortes in Cadiz was initially divided between liberals and those who wished to restore the Bourbon dynasty, it soon became clear that the appeal of the liberally oriented French could not be blunted unless new liberal laws were enacted. The threat of French influence, therefore, ensured that the liberals won out. Among the deputies of the Cortes, Raymond Carr (1966, 94) argues, there was "a widespread, if ill-defined, feeling for a constitution based on a division of powers, for uniform, modern laws, for civil equality, and the curtailment of corporate privilege."

The Cadiz Constitution was the most liberal constitution of the period. But since it never took full effect, its legacy lies less in its specific provisions than in the liberal ideas that informed it. Carr (1966, 96) notes that the Spanish liberalism of this period drew from a variety of sources:

the facts and necessities of the national rising; the commonplaces of the eighteenth-century natural law school and Montesquieu; the historically tinged constitutionalism and generalized feeling for reform that was characteristic of the Godoy epoch; the more radical brand of constituent reform that found strong press support in 1808; the influence and example of France; the works of Bentham.

The liberalism of Cadiz had implications for the Philippines. The Constitution designated American colonies and the Philippines as overseas provinces entitled to representation. And although the Constitution's eventual nullification would reverse this arrangement, the demand that the Philippines become a Spanish province entitled to representation continued until Rizal's time (Legarda 2011, 3).

Varela was a staunch defender of the liberalism of the Cortes and its constitution. At the request of the City of Manila in 1810, he composed instructions for Ventura de los Reyes, the representative of the Philippines to Cadiz. The instructions to de los Reyes, notes Joaquin (2005, 29), already contained reforms similar to those that Rizal would advocate later: Varela told de los Reyes to lobby for the establishment free schools outside friar control and the foundation of colleges for pharmacy, mathematics, and navigation. In 1813, Varela published a collection of verses entitled *Parnaso Filipino*. In its introduction, he defended the Cadiz Constitution, thereby drawing attacks from friars in the Philippines, who disdained the constitution for granting equal rights to natives of the Philippines, *indios* (ibid., 29).

The brief liberal interregnum in Spain ended with the restoration of Ferdinand VII to the throne in 1813. The Bourbon King nullified the constitution, jailed many of the Cadiz's liberal representatives, and broke his promise to convene a new Cortes—re-establishing an absolutist monarchy. In 1820, however, a mutiny in defense of the Cadiz Constitution broke out under the leadership of Col. Rafael de Riego. The three-year period of liberal rule under Riego, known as the *Trienio Liberal*, was another period of liberal promise cut short by French, who restored Ferdinand to the throne. Upon Ferdinand's return to power, he sentenced numerous liberals to death, including the parliamentary deputy for the Philippines, Vicente Posada (Sarkisyanz 1995, 80).

Ferdinand's second reign coincided with Spain losing its control over its Latin American colonies to creole radicals. The colonial government in the Philippines rightly suspected that creole radicalism would spread to the colony, and became increasingly wary of "Filipinos" (Spaniards born in the Philippines). In 1821, it uncovered a plot of creole military officers to overthrow the peninsular (Spaniards born in the peninsula)-led government. The Bayot Conspiracy, named after the Bayot brothers who led the movement, resulted in the government replacing many of the Mexican and creole officers with peninsulars. Despite this precaution, continued discontent led to an open revolt led by the Mexican Captain Andres Novales the following year. The mutineers killed the outgoing Governor General and proclaimed Novales "Emperor of the Philippines." But a swift counterattack allowed the government to crush the revolt and execute Novales within one day (Legarda 2011, 4). Fearing more revolts, the government deported many creoles to Spain, chief among them Varela, who was tagged a conspirator in Novales's revolt (ibid., 78).

The Bayot Conspiracy and the Novales Revolt are relevant because of their scope. They were not just local uprisings against colonial injustice, but movements that sought to liberate the entire colony from peninsular power. They proved that the creole advocacy for representative government had crystallized into the colony's first movement for independence (De Llobet 2009, 65).

Despite the increased suppression of liberalism in the metropole and creole radicalism in the colony, liberal ideas continued to circulate in Manila. In the 1820s, an English visitor, Henry Piddington, noted the clandestine circulation of works by Voltaire, Paine, and Rousseau among Manila-based progressive peninsulars and creoles, interested in South American revolutions (Corpuz 1989, 42). And while El Conde Filipino himself may have receded into obscurity, foreswearing his old republican commitments, prominent creole families such as the Regidors and the Pardo de Taveras constituted a small, yet influential, core of liberals in the colony (Joaquin 2005, 30).

Amid the steady, if uneven, spread of republican and liberal ideals in the Philippines, extreme reaction was also taking root. Ferdinand's death in 1833 led to a succession battle between his fourth wife, the Queen Regent Maria Cristina (representing her infant daughter Isabella II), and his brother Carlos V. To fend off Carlos's reactionary followers, Maria Cristina was forced to compromise with liberals, who once again regained influence during the period of Carlist uprising.

During the Carlist wars, reactionary Carlists moved to the colonies to escape moments of liberal triumph in Spain. In 1836, Spanish Prime Minister Jose Alvarez Mendizabal suppressed the religious orders, leading some to flee the metropole and move to the Philippines. As economic historian Benito Legarda notes (2011, 6), "Anti-clerical ideas plus fiscal necessity led to the confiscation of monastic properties." The following year, Philippine Governor General Pedro Antonio Salazar recommended that the government take advantage of the closing of monasteries to send 200 friars to man parishes in the Philippines (ibid., 6–7).

The dumping of friars brought some of the least talented and most reactionary priests to the colony—a process accelerated by the opening of the Suez Canal in 1869. If before only the dedicated traveled overseas, now the newly homeless friars relocated to the Philippines with relative ease (ibid., 7). Fleeing an increasingly anti-clerical and liberal Spain, many of them sought to rebuild their more traditional Spain in their new home, creating tensions between local clergy, who were mostly anti-Carlist and loyal to the reigning queen (Sarkisyanz 1995, 82–83). In an essay from 1889, Rizal himself decried the "reactionary Carlist friar" as the personification of everything he was against: a "mean egoist, tyrant, oppressor, enemy of all progress and lover of everything feudal, of everything absolute" (PHW, 79).

Friar control was not only political, but also economic. The orders received stipends proportionate to the number of citizens in their parishes, on top of the regular collections and contributions they received (Corpuz 1989, 120). And, as we shall see, their extensive land holdings ensured that they benefited from the export boom of the late nineteenth century.

The first major revolt against friar rule occurred in 1841. Objecting to a ban against natives (indios) joining the orders of friars, religious leader Apolonario dela Cruz, better known as Hermano Pule, set up his own order for indios, which quickly grew into the thousands. Suspecting a possible rebellion, the Spanish authorities suppressed the religious insurgents, leading to a violent confrontation that ended with Pule's execution. Unlike the Bayot Mutiny and the Novales Revolt, Hermano Pule's movement, composed of indios, not creoles, signified a shift in "the social complexion of dissent in the years from 1840 to 1880" (Mojares 2017, 28). Nevertheless, Pule's group received support from creoles known for engaging in anti-government activities, indicating a continuity between the proto-nationalist movements of the early nineteenth century (ibid.).

THE GLORIOUS REVOLUTION AND THE ECONOMIC BOOM YEARS

Two factors jolted liberal activity in the mid- to late nineteenth century. The first was the colony's export-fueled growth, and the second was the 1868 Glorious Revolution in Spain.

Wealth amid a stifling colonial government breeds resentment, and the Philippines was becoming wealthier and the government more stifling. As Joaquin (2005, 26) notes, "People become less and less willing to swallow slights as they become more and more wealthy and cultured." "A Rizal born in a mansion and educated in Europe," he adds, "is not going to kowtow to some ignorant small-town curate."

Manila opened to world trade in 1834, attracting foreign capital to the city. Foreigners introduced industrial machinery for sugar milling and rice hulling, increasing rice and sugar exports. After the removal of the government tobacco monopoly in 1882, exports in this sector followed suit (Schumacher 1997, 17). From 1825 to 1895, the colony's export earnings expanded from 1,000,000 pesos to 36,600,000 (Schumacher 1991, 17). At the close of the century, foreign trade accounted for 36% of GDP (Legarda 2011, 18). Because of increased trade, Manila in the late nineteenth century became a cosmopolitan hub, a port of call for ships from East Asia and as even the East Coast of the United States. As its wealth grew, it attracted a stream of mostly internal migrants, with its population increasing from 100,000 in 1822 to 150,000 by mid-century (Abinales and Amoroso 2017, 78).

Much of this wealth bypassed the Spanish and went to the hands of the domestic elite, who became partners of British trading companies and Chinese businessmen. "British and Chinese domination of imports, exports, and distribution," explain Abinales and Amoroso (2017, 80), "left little scope for Spaniards bereft of managerial experience or capital, and the country became known informally as an 'Anglo Chinese colony.'" Part of the revolutionary fervor of the period may be explained by the persistence of a weak Spanish colonial state, amid an increasingly wealthy and global indigenous upper class.

Although the Spanish state was able to capture some of this wealth through a tobacco monopoly (1782–1883), the Spaniards who benefited the most from the export boom were the friars, whose vast land holdings allowed them to profit from multiple cash crop exports such as rice, fruits, and vegetables (ibid.). The wealth and power of the friars were most evident in the Tagalog-speaking provinces near Manila, where almost 40% of the land was friar territory (ibid.). One such province was Laguna, home province of the Rizals. Because of the export boom, "their proximity to Manila," and "the improvements in irrigation dams and other facilities that their owners had built over the years," friar lands in provinces like Laguna, Bulacan, and Cavite became very valuable (Schumacher 1991, 11).[2]

Amid what Onofre Corpuz (1989, 41) calls a "century of progress" both economically and politically, the friar orders and peninsular Spaniards wished to govern by the rules of the eighteenth century. Even when a liberal government in Spain sent Spanish liberals to take positions in the colonial bureaucracy, they would be unable to govern without support from the friars. These liberals would, as a consequence, turn their backs on their liberal beliefs whenever the friars claimed that revolution was eminent (ibid.).

In 1868, another military revolution overthrew Isabella II, whose liberal sympathies had vacillated during the First Carlist War. In 1869, the Cortes promulgated another constitution with liberal provisions. Though its provisions did not apply to the Philippines, explains Corpuz (1989, 5), "Filipinos took encouragement from it and sought to campaign for equality in law and for civil and political rights." This campaign manifested in the creole-led Comite de Reformadores, which promoted the full assimilation of the Philippines under Spain. The Comite recruited students from the University of Santo Tomas, who organized the La Juventud Escolar Liberal (The Liberal Student Youth), which included Rizal's older brother, Paciano Mercado (later known as Paciano Rizal) (ibid., 5). Felipe Buencamino, a founding member of La Juventud Escolar Liberal, wrote that the Comite was the first "Liberal Party" in the Philippines, "composed of the richest and wisest Filipinos, causing very serious worry among the peninsular Spaniards especially among the friars" (quoted in ibid., 6).

These worries had been building up during the course of the Carlist war, as liberal ideas continued to flow from metropole to colony. Historian John Schumacher (1887, 11) speculates that "The deportations consequent upon the various coups prior to 1868 had brought a certain number of Liberal and Republican exiles to the country, who were, one may suppose, not completely silent about their ideas."

Further emboldening the local liberals was the arrival in 1869 of Governor General Carlos Maria de La Torre, who represented the post-revolutionary order in Spain. In July of that year, Manila residents led by members of the Comite feted La Torre by serenading him in the streets of Manila (Corpuz 1989, 8–9). La Torre attempted to implement liberal reforms such as the secularization of the Dominican-run University of

---

[2] It is not surprising that these same provinces would rise up in revolt in 1896.

Santo Tomas and the establishment of a public educational institute that would absorb secondary educational courses taught by religious order (ibid., 12). It was also a time of relaxed press censorship (Thomas 2012, 11). By 1871, however, a shift in the political climate in Madrid and the assassination of his political patron led to La Torre's dismissal (Corpuz 1989, 12). The liberal governor general did not change much. But, as Megan Thomas (2012, 11) explains, his legacy was not one "of long-lasting change but of the unforgettable taste of promise" Filipinos would come to expect more from their government.

THE CAVITE MUTINY

The concerns of the Comite de Reformadores reveal the contours of Philippine liberalism of the time. The Comite was divided into two sub-committees—one for lay members and another for priests (Corpuz 1989, 5)—indicating that one of its key concerns was the struggle for equal rights within the Catholic Church. By the late nineteenth century, native clergy had become more assertive against the friar orders, who had de facto monopoly over Philippine parishes. Since the Spanish colonial government expanded through churches, parishes served as the centers for community life in much of the colony. It was therefore unsurprising that a nationalist controversy would erupt from the issue of parish control.

In the 1770s, the crown ordered the "secularization" of the parishes, entailing a transfer of control from autonomous friar orders like the Dominicans and Franciscans (known as "regular clergy") to "secular" clergy under the jurisdiction of bishops. Initially, there were not enough secular clergy to govern the parishes. By the 1860s and 1870s, however, native priests had swelled the number of secular priests. Tensions were exacerbated by a ban on natives joining the friar orders.

The most significant propagandist prior to Rizal was the secular mestizo priest, Fr. Jose Burgos (1837–1872), a leading member of the Comite who advocated for the Filipinization of peninsular/friar-controlled parishes. In 1864, while only deacon, he wrote a manifesto by "the loyal Filipinos" addressed "to the noble Spanish Nation." In it, he used civil and canon law to argue that friars were disqualified from running parishes. More important was Burgos's identification as "Filipino"—a term which he used to refer to not only creoles but also Chinese mestizos and natives of the Philippines (Corpuz 1989, 3). This new meaning would become more common from this point onward, and, as we shall see, its racial inclusiveness would be key in Rizal's own thinking.

By the time of La Torre's arrival, Burgos had become the leader of the country's secular priests, by then the most important political grouping in the colony. The advocacy of the local priesthood was not only tied to the native and creole elite, it also represented the increasing identification of various racial groups with a common cause. Natives, creoles, and mestizos were all advocating for the secularization of the parishes (ibid., 14). If the government wished to disrupt the burgeoning of Filipino militancy, the secular priests were an ideal target.

In January 1872, troops in a garrison in the province of Cavite launched a mutiny, protesting the increased taxation ordered by the new Governor General. Like previous uprisings, it was quickly put down (ibid., 19). But despite its lack of military consequence, it served as a pretext for the arrest of many liberals whom the authorities accused of conspiring with the rebels (ibid. 21). The repression climaxed with the public garroting of Burgos and two other secular priests—Mariano Gomes and Jacinto Zamora—on February 17. It also led to the jailing and eventual exile of many Manila-based liberals, ending a long period of liberal agitation.

Burgos and the generation of 1872 served as inspirations for Rizal. Writing to fellow propagandist Mariano Ponce, Rizal, speaking in the third person, claimed that "without 1872 Rizal would be a Jesuit now and instead of writing *Noli me Tangere*, would have written the opposite." Seeing the injustice committed to Burgos and his fellow priests, Rizal's "imagination was awakened," swearing to "devote myself to avenge one day so many victims, and with this idea in mind I have been studying and this can be read in all my works and writings" (Reformists, 321).

THE RISE OF THE ILUSTRADO

The liberal-nationalist movement would remain dormant after 1872 and would not re-emerge until Rizal and his cohort became adults. As Joaquin (2005, 37) explains, the rise to prominence of Rizal's generation "signified three things: the convalescence of the Philippine middle class after the crisis of '72; the rise in it of a new, non-Creole leadership; and the emergence of the Filipino into the modern world."

It was during the late nineteenth century that the term "ilustrado" came to refer to educated Filipinos—initially creoles, but increasingly also natives—who advocated for the liberal reforms of earlier intellectuals like

Varela. The ilustrado, of which Rizal would become the most prominent example, was, explains Caroline S. Hau (2017, 128), a "slippery" identity. It was not a simple marker of class, because very many educated men from Manila were not rich. It was also not racial because many ilustrados were neither Spanish mestizo nor creole. And it was also unclear what level of educational attainment was necessary to be designated "ilustrado" (ibid., 129). Rather than proposing a strict definition, Hau posits that *ilustrado* signified a critical enlightened stance. She notes that "The etymology of the word plays on the metaphor of 'light' in the 'enlightenment,' holding up knowledge (via education) against the 'darkness' of ignorance, error, and obscurantism." The term was therefore linked to "words like *liberal, progresista, reformista* or *reformador, librepensador* (often appearing in the English form, 'freethinker'), *volteriano* (Volterian), and, most famously, *filosofo* and *filibustero*" (ibid., 130).

Many ilustrados moved to Spain, forming an expatriate movement that basked in the relative freedoms of Europe. Their port of entry was Barcelona, a center of Spanish liberalism and radicalism. From there, they went to Madrid and other European cities, making friends with European liberals and republicans along the way (Corpuz 1989, 66). In Spain, they gained allies among Spanish liberal republicans like the Mason and leading Cadiz-era politician Miguel Morayta, philosopher Rafael Maria de Labra, and even the president of the short-lived Spanish republic, the Catalan federalist Francisco Pi Y Margall (ibid.).

The main organ of late ilustrado thought was the newspaper *La Solidaridad* (1889–1895). Committed to Enlightenment and progress, the paper "aimed to air liberal ideas in politics, science, arts, commerce, and other fields" (Mojares 2006, 456). It was also internationalist in its outlook, covering Latin American and European, and Asian politics, with correspondents in Havana, New York, and Saigon. In particular, it focused on the theme of solidarity between the Philippines and other Spanish "overseas provinces" like Cuba and Puerto Rico (ibid., 456). Its stated goal was:

> To combat all reaction and all backward steps; to applaud and accept every liberal idea and to defend progress; in a word, to be a propagandist first and foremost of all democratic ideals, hoping that these may reign in all nations here and beyond the seas. (Quoted in Corpuz 1989, 170)

The Filipino ilustrados thrived in the small secretive organizations that anchored much of liberal politics in turn-of-the-century Spain. Most of them, Rizal included, were Masons, and as Schumacher (1991, 5) notes, Masonry became a major "vehicle for the articulation of liberal ideals" and the ilustrado vision of a national community. For the ilustrado Mariano Ponce, Masonry served as "a school which would provide [our people] with models for cooperative action and accustom it to live as a collectivity" (quoted in ibid.).

One would think the Comite and its La Juventud Escolar Liberal had reconstituted itself in Europe, with the exiles lobbying for the assimilation that these groups campaigned for decades before. And like their forebears, they too would celebrate the blurring of racial boundaries. In describing his group of expatriates, Rizal noted, "They are creole young men of Spanish descent, Chinese half-breeds, and Malayans; but we call ourselves only Filipino" (Letters to Blumentritt, 72). This was an aspiration more than a reality, as there was always political infighting between creoles and indios within the Philippine colony. Nevertheless, it signified a vision for multiracial nationalism that would become integral to Rizal's thinking.

The overseas propaganda movement therefore linked Rizal and his cohort not just to European liberalism and republicanism; it likewise connected them to the Philippine liberalism of the Comite Reformadores, the first liberal party of the country. Rizal's life occurred at the intersection of various liberal currents.

RIZAL'S LIFE

Jose Rizal Mercado y Alonso was born on June 19, 1861, "five years after Freud, four years after Conrad, one year after Chekov, the same year as Tagore, three years before Max Weber, five years before Sun Yat-sen, eight years before Gandhi, and nine before Lenin," (Anderson 1998, 227) to a sugarcane planter family in the town of Calamba, province of Laguna. The province is just outside Manila, and its residents are part of the dominant Tagalog-speaking area in a multilingual country. The Rizals (then known as the Mercados) were not landowners, but leaseholders of friar lands. Given the export boom of the period, however, even these leaseholders, called *inquilinos*, became increasingly wealthy.

Both Rizal's parents were educated in Manila, and his paternal grandfather was a provincial governor. On his mother's side, a few relatives were minor government officials and a few were lawyers or priests (Schumacher 1997, 33).

Rizal's political awakening occurred in 1872, the year of the Cavite Mutiny. Like another nineteenth-century militant, Lenin, one of Rizal's earliest political influences was his brother, Paciano Mercado—a leading member of the Juventud Escolar Liberal, who was a witness to the repression of the period. After the execution of the secular priests in 1872, Rizal recalled that Paciano "had to leave the University, as he was a liberal and the friars did not like him for having lived with Burgos." At the time, Rizal was about to move to Manila for his studies, so to not "encounter great obstacles in my studies, he [Paciano] advised me to use our second name which is Rizal" (Letters to Blumentritt 1, 265). "Therefore I am the only Rizal, because at home my parents, my sisters, and my brothers, and my relatives have always preferred the old surname *Mercado*." "In this way," he quipped, "it seems that I am an illegitimate son!" (ibid.).

As the government cracked down on the liberals, Rizal moved to Manila for secondary education at the Jesuit-run Ateneo Municipal, then considered the finest colegio in the colony. Here, he perfected his Spanish and obtained a classical education in mathematics, literature, rhetoric, and the natural sciences. His years under the Jesuits would be the happiest of his life, and he developed a deep bond with the religious order that remained even after he became a critic of the Catholic Church (his novels are notable for exempting Jesuits from their opprobrium).

After completing his bachelor degree in 1877, he commenced university studies with the Dominicans at the University of Santo Tomas. After studying metaphysics for one year, he proceeded to take preparatory courses in medicine. While he would later excel as a physician, he did not have the aptitude for medicine that he had for the arts, and he distracted himself with courses more suited to his talents (Bernad 1986, 38–39). Over his four years as a medical student in Santo Tomas, he continued studying painting, music, and literature outside the university (ibid., 36).

In 1882, Rizal cut his time at Santo Tomas short to study in Spain. His trip was a secret, and it was only as he was about to board a ship that he sent a telegram to his parents telling them of his departure (ibid., 43). The plan was likely hatched by Paciano, who would supply Rizal's stipend. The reasons for Rizal's secrecy are vague, but Schumacher (1997, 36) notes that the voyage to Europe was not intended for career advancement, but "as a means of fulfilling a patriotic mission, or of preparing himself to do something for his country."

After spending a summer in Barcelona, Rizal moved to Madrid, where he spent three years obtaining two separate licenses—one in medicine from the Colegio de San Carlos and another in philosophy and letters from the Universidad Central (Bernad 1986, 52–53). Though he exhibited competency in his medical studies, he once again excelled in the arts, where he won awards such as first prize in Greek literature (ibid., 52).

The years 1886 and 1887 were spent in Paris and Heidelberg as an ophthalmologist in training. It was during this period that Rizal began corresponding with Ferdinand Blumentritt, an orientalist from the Oberrealschule (he was the equivalent of a secondary school teacher) in the present-day Czech Republic. From this point on, it was the Austrian who would guide Rizal's readings in history, anthropology, and linguistics (ibid., 58). He would also introduce Rizal to a network of European scholars interested in the Philippines (ibid., 59).

In March 1887, Rizal published *Noli me Tangere* in Berlin, after which he returned to the Philippines in August 1887, where the novel was roundly condemned by friars. He would stay there until January of the following year, departing once again for Europe amid the controversy generated by his work (see Chap. 3).

After traveling through Hong Kong, Japan, and the United States, Rizal crossed the Atlantic to London, where he engaged in historical research. The result of this work was an annotation of Antonio de Morga's 1609 account, *Sucesos de las Islas Filipinas*, which he used to paint of picture of precolonial Tagalog society.[3] From London, he stayed in Paris for a year, and moved Brussels for a few months. In 1891, he published his second novel, *El Filibusterismo*.

Rizal's time in Europe was his most productive, and it was there that he produced the bulk of his political work. But tensions within the expatriate movement and a crisis in his home province drew him back home. In 1887, the Mercados and other inquilinos of Calamba were engaged in bitter disputes with their Dominican landlords. The friars were not only extending their territory, but also demanding more rent from tenants, leading to a few forcible evictions. Rizal himself orchestrated the resistance during an earlier visit, and his brother and brothers-in-law continued the campaign. It was a long and bitter legal struggle, given a complex system of land tenure that precluded easy resolution (Schumacher 1997, 246–247).

---

[3] Due to the introductory nature of this volume and the fact that it focuses on Rizal's political thought, I will not be unable to devote much space to this historical/ethnological work. Interested readers may refer to the work of Filomeno Aguilar (2005), which remains the best critical examination of Rizal's annotation of Morga's work.

Back in Europe, the expatriates lobbied to elevate the dispute to courts in Spain (ibid., 248). They viewed this legal struggle as part of their broader campaign for the recognition of Philippine concerns in Spain. But their campaign would have little effect on the Philippines as the authoritarian Governor General Valeriano Weyler threw his full support at the friars. By the beginning of 1890, the provincial government of Calamba had deported Paciano, two of his brothers-in-law, and two other relatives to the island of Mindoro (ibid., 249).

The events in his hometown solidified Rizal's belief that an independence movement would one day be necessary. He had also grown disillusioned with the expatriate movement, writing in 1891 of the "general error" that Filipino propagandists could promote their cause while "in a distant country" (Reformists, 629). "Medicine," he argued, "should be brought near to the patient" (ibid., 629–630). "The battlefield," he concluded, was the Philippines. "There we will help one another, there together we will suffer on triumph perhaps" (ibid., 630). Rizal knew returning would prove dangerous and he had visions of martyrdom early. Writing to Blumentritt from Ghent in September 1891, he said, "I have to return to the Philippines. Life is becoming a burden to me here. I have to give an example not to fear death, even if this may be terrible" (Letters to Blumentritt, 416).

Rizal's resolve to return was solidified by growing tensions with *La Solidaridad*'s Marcelo del Pilar over the leadership of the Philippine colony. Though much of the tension was personal, part of it also reflected Rizal's growing detachment from the movement of overseas propaganda. Shortly after completing *El Filibusterismo*, he departed Europe for Hong Kong, where he practiced medicine while living with his family in self-imposed exile from December 1891 to June 1892. Rizal was happy in Hong Kong, and even considered settling permanently. Indeed, Hong Kong had already been a comfortable place of exile for Filipinos who had been forced to flee after the Cavite Mutiny. But politics would draw him back to his country (Guerrero 2012, 320).

In Hong Kong, Rizal stayed in touch with many of his former colleagues in Europe, who consulted him with on various points of policy (ibid., 320). He wrote for English newspapers about the events in Calamba and prepared propaganda leaflets for distribution in the Philippines, including translations of his articles and the French Declaration of the Rights of Man (Schumacher 1997, 270). He also struggled with a third novel, which he had attempted to write in Tagalog and not Spanish (ibid.,

321).[4] And he began thinking of creating a colony for the refugees of Calamba province in British North Borneo—an idea that received endorsement from the British authorities (Bernad 1986, 76–77).

Most importantly, in Hong Kong Rizal began to draft the statutes of a movement he would call *La Liga Filipina*. Although ostensibly a peaceful mutual aid organization that sought to unite the archipelago in the cause of reform, there is evidence that Rizal saw the *Liga* as a vehicle for an independence movement, with one member testifying that the organization had been set up to raise money for an armed insurrection (Guerrero 2012, 332). Though we cannot be sure of its ultimate intent, it is likely that Rizal viewed the *Liga* as a new phase in the liberal-nationalist movement. If the first phase was represented by Burgos and the Comite, and the second phase was the expatriate movement, the *Liga* would be its third and possibly final.

Rizal returned to Manila on June 26, 1892, and promptly organized the *Liga* within one week of arrival. In the Manila district of Tondo, "A small group of liberals and progressives, almost all of them Masons, had gathered" to listen to Rizal outline the principles of his new organization (ibid., 347). It was an open meeting, with little security, yet some witnesses claim that it was here that Rizal openly called for the formation of an independence movement (ibid.).

Oddly, it was not political organizing that landed Rizal in jail, but anti-Catholic publications he had allegedly smuggled into the country through his sister's luggage (likely planted). His arrest would lead to his exile in the far-flung Dapitan in the southern island Mindanao, where he would spend the next four years. There, he stayed away from political agitation, working instead on local projects such as building a school and even a water system. It was in Dapitan where he met and fell in love with Josephine Bracken, a resident of Hong Kong who had accompanied her adoptive father to see Rizal for treatment. He may have found peace, but the years in Dapitan, notes biographer Austin Coates (1992, 283), were "like a slowly closing vice bent upon reducing his morale to its lowest possible point, at which moment, and in which state, he would be called upon to undergo the supreme and final test, his trial and execution."

---

[4] Rizal's struggles are similar to many present-day Filipino intellectuals who are more comfortable with English than Tagalog. See Ocampo, 1992, for an account of Rizal's incomplete third novel.

The Cuban Revolution broke out in February 1895. Barely a year after, the Filipinos led by the Katipunan would follow suit. In early 1896, the revolutionary Katipunan's leader, Andres Bonifacio, sent an emissary to Rizal to tell him about the imminent revolution and to seek his counsel. Hearing that the Katipunan had limited financial and military resources and foreseeing failure, Rizal advised against the uprising (ibid., 276).[5]

Meanwhile, Rizal, upon the prodding of Blumentritt, had hatched a plan to free himself from lonely exile. Toward the end of 1895, Rizal sent a letter to the Governor General volunteering for military service in Cuba (ibid., 274). In July of 1896, he received a positive reply from the Governor General, inviting him to become a medical officer. He was unenthusiastic about the plan—viewing it only as a convenient exit—but his growing depression, his sister's insistence on him leaving, and the solicitous tone of the Governor General's letter convinced him to depart (ibid., 278). As Rizal commenced his long trip to Cuba, revolution in the Philippines broke out.

In August 1896, the Spanish authorities discovered the existence of the Katipunan. Bonifacio had called for a national uprising, and on August 30, he launched a failed attack on a Spanish fort in the outskirts of Manila (ibid., 286). At this time, Rizal was in a cruiser in the province of Cavite, awaiting departure from Cuba (ibid., 283). Looking at Manila from across the water, Rizal wrote in his diary, "Pray God there will be no more disturbances this night. Unhappy countrymen who so madly plunge themselves to death" (quoted in ibid., 287).

By the end of the month, Rizal was on his way to Europe. Despite receiving a warning in Singapore that he was not safe, he refused to disembark from the ship. A day after departing from Port Said on September 28, the captain informed him that he would be arrested in Barcelona upon orders of the Governor General (ibid., 288). He was imprisoned briefly in Monjuich and then sent back to Manila (ibid., 290).

We will turn to Rizal's trial and his relationship with the revolution in succeeding chapters. For now, it is enough to note that, despite his categorical repudiation of the revolution, he had become the main inspiration for the revolutionaries. Moreover, his *La Liga Filipina*, of which Bonifacio was a member, may have led to the formation of the Katipunan, which

---

[5] As we shall see in the next chapter, this repudiation became the basis for radical historians to dismiss Rizal as a reformist critic of revolution. It is clear, however, that Rizal's primary objection centered on viability and not principle.

claimed Rizal as its honorary president, displayed his photograph in its meetings, and used his name as one of its secret passwords. In fact, the Katipunan (the name of the organization is closest Tagalog translation for the Spanish word "liga") may be viewed as a radical splinter group of *La Liga Filipina* that expanded the *Liga*'s Masonic, ilustrado base to include the urban middle class and, eventually, elements of the provincial gentry. These connections would allow the Spanish colonial government to convict Rizal for rebellion, sedition, and conspiracy, leading to Rizal's execution by firing squad on December 30, 1896.

Conclusion

Jose Rizal's emergence as the key liberal figure in Philippine history had numerous antecedents. In his life and works, we see the continuation of the earlier liberalism of creole intellectuals like Varela, who were inspired by the French Revolution and the liberal Cadiz Constitution. We also see the continuation of the proto-nationalism of Filipino clergymen like Jose Burgos. But Rizal also represented the flowering of liberalism among Filipino natives, showing that liberal principles could bind different racial groups through one goal. It was in this sense that liberal principles inaugurated the nationalist movement in the Philippines. Without a common rhetoric centered on rights and freedoms, creoles, indios, and mestizos would be unable to see themselves as a people.

In the next chapter, I examine not only how Rizal viewed liberalism as a binding rhetoric. I also discuss the conditions under which Rizal thought liberalism could blossom.

Bibliography

Abinales, Patricio N., and Donna J. Amoroso. 2017. *State and Society in the Philippines.* 2nd ed. Quezon City: Ateneo de Manila University Press.

Aguilar, Filomeno V. 2005. Tracing Origins: Ilustrado Nationalism and the Racial Science of Migration Waves. *The Journal of Asian Studies* 64 (03): 605–637.

Anderson, Benedict R.O'G. 1983. *Imagined Communities: Reflections on the Origin and Spread of Nationalism.* London/New York: Verso.

———. 1998. *The Spectre of Comparisons: Nationalism, Southeast Asia, and the World.* New York: Verso.

Bernad, Miguel A. 1986. *Rizal and Spain: An Essay in Biographical Context.* Metro Manila: National Book Store.

Carr, Raymond. 1966. *Spain, 1808–1939.* Oxford: Clarendon Press.

Coates, Austin. 1992. *Rizal, Philippine Nationalist and Martyr*. Manila: Solidaridad Publishing House.

Corpuz, O.D. 1989. *The Roots of the Filipino Nation, Volume II*. Quezon City: Aklahi Foundation, Inc.

De Llobet, Ruth. 2009. El Poeta, El Regidor y La Amante: Manila y La Emergencia de Una Identidad Criolla Filipina. *Istor: Revista de Historia Internacional* 38: 65–92.

Guerrero, Leon Ma. 2012. *The First Filipino: A Biography of Jose Rizal*. Makati City: Guerrero Publishing.

Hau, Caroline S. 2017. *Elites and Ilustrados in Philippine Culture*. Quezon City: Ateneo de Manila University Press.

Joaquin, Nick. 2005. *A Question of Heroes*. Pasig City: Anvil Publishing Inc.

Kirsch, Adam. 2016. Melancholy Liberalism. *City Journal*, Winter. http://www.city-journal.org/2016/26_1_melancholy-liberalism.html

Legarda, Benito. 2011. The Economic Background of Rizal's Time. *The Philippine Review of Economics* XLVIII (2): 1–22.

Mojares, Resil B. 2006. *Brains of the Nation: Pedro Paterno, T.H. Pardo de Tavera, Isabelo de Los Reyes and the Production of Modern Knowledge*. Quezon City: Ateneo de Manila University Press.

———. 2017. *Interrogations in Philippine Cultural History: The Ateneo de Manila Lectures*. Quezon City: Ateneo de Manila University Press.

Ocampo, Ambeth. 1992. *Makamisa: The Search for Rizal's Third Novel*. Pasig: Anvil Publishing Inc.

Polasky, Janet. 2015. *Revolutions Without Borders: The Call to Liberty in the Atlantic World*. New Haven: Yale University Press.

Rafael, Vicente L. 2015. Introduction: Revolutionary Contradictions. In *Luzon at War: Contradictions in Philippine Society, 1898–1902*, ed. Milagros Camayon Guerrero, 1–19. Mandaluyong City: Anvil Publishing Inc.

Sarkisyanz, Manuel. 1995. *Rizal and Republican Spain and Other Rizalist Essays*. Manila: National Historical Institute.

Schumacher, John N. 1991. *The Making of a Nation: Essays on Nineteenth-Century Filipino Nationalism*. Quezon City: Ateneo de Manila University Press.

———. 1997. *The Propaganda Movement: 1880–1895: The Creation of a Filipino Consciousness, the Making of a Revolution*. Quezon City: Ateneo de Manila University Press.

Thomas, Megan C. 2012. *Orientalists, Propagandists, and Ilustrados: Filipino Scholarship and the End of Spanish Colonialism*. Minneapolis/London: University of Minnesota Press.

CHAPTER 2

Pain and the Purification of Liberty

Abstract This chapter outlines the key ideas of Rizal's liberalism, drawing mostly from his essays and collected letters. Although Rizal believed that Spanish liberals were better than the reactionary friars whom he held in contempt, he felt that many of them had become hypocritical in the Philippines, turning their back on their principles. In opposition to this liberalism, Rizal sketches a form of liberalism born through the pain and suffering of the colonial subject.

Keywords Liberalism • Rizal • Liberty • Pain • Colonial • Rights • Revolution

Rizal viewed liberalism as "a plant that never dies" (PHW 15). He did not explain the metaphor, but we can guess what he meant. Like a plant, liberalism grows gradually, and, given the right conditions, it can display radiant color. Like a plant, liberalism also has different shades, and grows at different times, in different places. The period spanning the late eighteenth century and nineteenth century was a crucial time in liberalism's global history. But different liberal plants of this era grew in different places, at different paces, and were cultivated by different people. Some of these plants grew almost indefinitely, while others withered quickly. Liberalism, like many plants, is delicate, easily damaged, and prone to wilting.

© The Author(s) 2019
L. E. Claudio, *Jose Rizal*, Global Political Thinkers,
https://doi.org/10.1007/978-3-030-01316-5_2

The metaphor is apt but limited. For during this period the challenge that liberalism placed on established monarchies and clerical power would not have seemed like the gentle growing of a plant. The turn of the century was tempestuous, and this was largely because of liberals and their revolutions. The historian Eric Hobsbawm (1996) notes in the title of his classic account that the late eighteenth century was an "Age of Revolution"—a time when the Industrial Revolution altered methods of production, while the French and American revolutions shifted the tenor of political discourse.

The revolutions happened in Europe and North America, but liberal intellectual networks were not limited to Europe and North America. As Janet Polasky (2015, 2) shows, the "cry of liberty" of the late eighteenth century was a trans-Atlantic one—a revolutionary message shared by propagandists and pamphleteers in Europe, the Americas, the Caribbean, and Africa. By the early nineteenth century, Richard J. Evans (2016, 17) explains, "The liberals and revolutionaries driven into exile by reactionary regimes of the Restoration formed a kind of radical international whose connections spanned the Atlantic."

Liberalism is borderless and liberty universal, because tyranny is universal. The tension between tyrannical concentrations of power and individual liberty underlies all the many definitions of liberalism, and, as we shall see, it was crucial to Rizal's own interpretation. For is not colonialism tyranny writ large and nationalism a response to that tyranny? To quote Evans (2016, 178) once more, nationalism in nineteenth-century Europe became a "means to bring about liberal and political and constitutional reform" amid the reaction of empires. This was the case in Europe, the Americas, and the Atlantic world more broadly, but we can make similar observations in other, colonial settings. If it is true that nationalism and liberalism shared a common grammar in the nineteenth century, how might this inform our assessment of anti-colonial nationalists from this period?

By the late nineteenth century, liberalism had sealed its alliance with the bourgeois, and most liberals took for granted the need to preserve property rights, ushering in what Hobsbawm (1997, 15) referred to as an "age of capital," a time of a "massive advance of the world economy of industrial capitalism, of the social order it represented, of the ideas and beliefs which seemed to legitimize and ratify it: in reason, science, progress and liberalism." At the turn of the century, moreover, the era's capitalism had expanded to various colonies in what Hobsbawm (1989) then called an "age of empire." Alas, the defender of liberalism cannot deny that liberals played a key role in the imperialism of this period. As Uday Singh Mehta (1999) has shown, liberal ideas of progress, particularly in Britain, became the basis through which imperialists judged non-Western peoples as backward and premodern. The universalism of thinkers such as like J.S. Mill allowed liberals to construct a linear vision of politics that they were willing to impose on non-Western peoples.

Certain strains of liberalism did turn oppressive and pro-colonial in places like London. But liberalism kept its insurgent, revolutionary character in the Philippines, partly because the see-saw of politics in Spain kept Spanish liberals both outside and inside the halls of power. As we saw in the previous chapter, the ideas of the French Revolution and the Constitution of Cadiz slowly percolated in the colony, turning revolutionary at the close of the century. This chapter seeks to capture the radicalism inherent in Rizal's liberalism. In particular, it outlines a key element of Rizal's liberalism in the colony, namely, that pain and suffering purify one's liberalism.

A SUPERIOR LIBERALISM

When Rizal and his generation of intellectuals articulated a liberalism for the colony, they did so with an awareness of liberalism's failings in Europe. They also knew that many European liberals—especially the Spaniards in the Philippines—refused to see the need for liberty in colonial contexts. For Rizal, the Enlightenment was consistently blocked in his country by the obscurantism of the friar orders and hypocritical Spanish "liberals" who abetted them. Rizal and his cohort would in turn claim the mantle of liberalism for themselves and experiment with a new form adapted to their political needs.

Such audacity was expected of them. The ilustrados, as Megan C. Thomas (2012, 4) argues, were "worldly colonials," who drew knowledge from not only Spain but the broader European Enlightenment. They saw themselves as superior, more cosmopolitan, than the Spaniards who lorded over their backward country. "These young colonial subjects," explains Thomas, "positioned themselves as modern scholars and intellectuals in a broader field in which their colonizers, the Spanish, often lagged behind. For them, the world of scholarship had "no political boundaries or authority, but only the authority of reason and evidence" (ibid.). Such an attitude explains why ilustrados learned multiple languages and studied in multiple European centers of learning. Thus the colonials did not just view their modernity as a parallel modernity to Spanish modernity. In many ways, they thought theirs was advanced.

Thomas's work focuses on the ilustrado assertion of worldly superiority in areas such as anthropology, linguistics, and historiography. But the ilustrados likewise saw themselves as superior to their Spanish oppressors in the sphere of political philosophy. Rizal would have thought himself a better liberal than Spaniards who passed off as "progressive" in backward, colonial Philippines, for he had honed his liberalism through interactions with Spain's great republicans, who, unlike the Spaniards in the Philippines, treated him and his colleagues as intellectual equals. He would have also seen himself as more steeped in the literature of the liberal tradition, having traveled to places like Paris, London, and New York.

Rizal could be both ham-fisted and subtle when defending liberalism and the Enlightenment in the colony. On the one hand, there is his didactic sculpture "El Triunfo de la Muerte Sobre la Vida" (The Triumph of Death over Life), which depicts a skeletal symbol of death embracing a dead woman who symbolizes Enlightenment. On the other hand, there are the numerous satirical descriptions of "liberal" professionals in his novels, like that of the influence-peddler and government advisor Don Custodio in *El Filibusterismo*, who "wanted to get through it all and still give everyone what they wanted" (*Fili*, 166). Custodio represented the liberal in colonial settings, whose appetite for power had made him a hypocrite willing to compromise on liberalism's core values (see Chap. 4).

Can liberals be mere arbitrators and still call themselves liberals? To some extent, they can, because as John Gray (2000, 2) explains, liberalism has two faces. Because it is rooted in the Enlightenment, its first face seeks an "ideal way of life" based on "universal principles." Its second face, however, seeks "terms of peace among different ways of life." In this regard, liberalism is likewise a modus vivendi (ibid.).

There is a sense that liberalism in Rizal's Philippines had swung too much toward its second face, with arbiters like the fictional Don Custodio and the various "liberal" peninsular officials who confused compromise with opportunism. Liberalism's two faces are in constant tension, and Rizal and his cohort aimed to restore liberalism's claims on universal values. For how could Enlightenment values be truly universal if they were inapplicable to a colony? In trying to make the universal truly universal, Rizal's aim was a purification of liberalism. If there were to be a "genuine" liberalism, it was to be found in those who were most denied their liberties.

First Principles

The national hero of the Philippines is, naturally, known in his country for his nationalism. But, as Rizal's foremost biographer Leon Ma. Guerrero (2013, 56) explains, Rizal was first a liberal, "seeking for himself and the Filipinos the legal and constitutional rights of the Spaniards; it was only in resignation, in despair, that he became a nationalist." Like European nationalists of the period, Rizal saw nationalism as an escape from the reaction inherent in the ancien regime.

As an Enlightenment thinker, Rizal's main preoccupation was social progress, and he equated this progress with liberalism. In a letter to Blumentritt where he narrates an argument he had with former Jesuit teachers, he claims that the Jesuits, though more enlightened than the friars, did not march "at the head of progress" because they did not "accept the liberal principles of progress" (Letters to Blumentritt, 328). These principles were basic rights like "freedom of the press, freedom of thought, freedom of religion (ibid.)"—rights-based liberalism at its simplest. Today, we would say that Rizal's liberalism placed a premium on defending civil liberties.

The main barrier to the rights Rizal sought was the colonial system and its most reactionary representatives, the friars. In an essay from 1889, he wrote: "We shout very loudly that the friars at this historic moment are detrimental to the national interest in the Philippines, because they are an obstacle to the introduction of any kind of liberal reforms which are urgently and peremptorily needed" (PHW, 81). The friars were barriers to forward-looking education, a key tenet of Rizal's civic liberalism. Because they opposed the teaching of the Spanish language, Filipino students were unable to "read the beautiful stories and theories of liberty, progress, and justice" and "understand the laws, know our rights and then find in practice other laws and other things different from them" (ibid., 11). In Rizal's novels, friars were not only hypersexualized and avaricious, but constant hindrances to any kind of reform.

Without any liberty, the presence of Spain in the Philippines would be pointless. "Spain," Rizal continued, "did not plant in those Islands the invincible standard of Castile so that they might be the exclusive patrimony and feudal dominion of the reactionary friars but rather assimilate and equalize them." He demanded from Spain the "precious gifts" of "liberty, rights, social as well as political," which formed the "inestimable legacy of the French Revolution, systematically anathematized by the friars to the country's misfortune" (ibid.).

Realizing that his early advocacy for Filipinos to be granted full rights as Spanish citizens was impossible, he began to aspire for an independent nation. Though he was ambivalent about the Philippine revolution, his writings set the stage for the revolutionaries of the Katipunan, which called him their honorary president and used his name as a rallying cry. The liberal Rizal inspired the first anti-colonial revolution in Asia.

That a liberal inspired a revolution may sound absurd today, but this would not have been the case in the nineteenth century. Prior to the emergence of ethno-nationalism in Bismarck's Prussia, most nationalist revolutions in Europe were either launched or inspired by liberal thinkers. Rizal was no different from the European liberals of his era, and his writings abound with liberal demands like a free press, fair taxation, the end of forced labor, and democratic representation. It is not coincidental that in 1891, while in Hong Kong preparing to return to the Philippines after years in Europe, he was translating the French Declaration of the Rights of Man—the source text of European liberalism—for readers in the Philippines (Schumacher 1997, 270). Rizal was conscious of the liberal heritage of Philippine nationalism and dreamed of creating an independent nation animated by visions of liberty.

Rizal was no different from many nationalist liberals of the period. One may, in fact, understand Rizal through comparisons with leading European thinkers of the century like the apostle of Italian unification, Giuseppe Mazzini (1805–1872). A textbook description of the Italian's politics can be just as easily be used to describe the Filipino's:

> Mazzini was both a romantic and a liberal. As a liberal, he fought for republican and constitutional government and held that national unity would enhance individual liberty. As a romantic, he sought truth through heightened feeling and intuition and believed that an awakened Italy would lead to the regeneration of humanity. (Perry et al. 2009, 600)

But if Rizal was simply an Asian Mazzini, what sets his ideas apart? The answer lies in his context. Nineteenth-century Europeans were often fighting monarchies and reactionary empires. Rizal, however, was struggling against a colonial system that projected itself from Europe to a place halfway around the world—a colonial system that would receive the tacit support of liberals in the metropole. Moreover, this colonial system was an exhaust valve for reactionaries who could no longer thrive in Europe. When liberalism seemed triumphant in Europe, nothing would change in the colony, since it served as a dumping ground for the Carlist friars that Rizal despised. In such a context, contradictions and even hypocrisies become more evident. In such a context, liberalism easily fails. But in such a context, liberalism may also be purified.

LIBERTY AND PAIN

This book's main argument is that Rizal's liberalism for the colonized was premised on a relationship with political pain: Liberty is earned through suffering. As John Schumacher (1997, 253) notes, Rizal's "belief that suffering is part if the price to be paid for national redemption underscores his firm confidence in the ultimate victory of courage and virtue over injustice." To fight injustice, Rizal mined the Enlightenment for an alternative vision of his country's future. His sources were varied, but his education led him to study great European thinkers from the great Spanish polemicist Mariano de Larra to Victor Hugo. Rizal was unlike many Asian nationalists of today, who obsess over the provenance of ideas rather than assessing their political usefulness. If a writer illumined a universal truth, Rizal accepted the challenge of grappling with this truth for his nation.

But his admiration for European liberalism did not mean he admired the Spanish liberals in the Philippines. In his letters and novels, he often portrayed Spanish liberals as feckless, too quick to give up on their ideals. By contrast, a Filipino liberalism would be more virtuous—a return to first principles.

The most crucial text that defines Rizal's thoughts on liberalism in the Philippines is the 1890 essay "How the Philippines Is Governed"—an essay that, to my knowledge, has yet to be discussed at length. In it, Rizal outlines a major cleavage in the governance of Philippine society, one that pits Spanish friars with Spanish liberals in government. On the one hand, he notes that the friars "attribute all the ills of the country to the liberal ministers who, for being liberals, must be ignorant." They then credit the little good in Philippine society "to themselves; the reactionary ministers or those from the convent who solely for being so, are wise, do neither good nor ill" (PHW, 288).

On the other hand, "Spanish liberal elements in the Philippines blame the friars for the backwardness of the Philippines and rightly so, inasmuch as governing them as the convents do govern them, the blame for the disorder must fall upon them" (ibid., 289). Naturally, Rizal was sympathetic to the Spanish liberals, and knew how they were beacons of hope for reform-minded Filipinos. Rizal would have been aware, for example, of how these Filipinos once feted the liberal Governor General Carlos Maria de La Torre (see Chap. 1). But the increasingly pro-independence Rizal had started to give up on Spanish liberals, whom he felt had compromised much of their principles in the colony. Spanish liberals, he contended, "forget the part they have in the disorder," and he would not allow them to wash their hands of their responsibility, claiming:

> If they do not allow themselves to be governed and to be used as tools as it often happens; if for fear of losing their jobs they do not compromise in many things that are repugnant to their convictions; *if they have more firmness, more faith in their ideals*, if they study the country more and they try earnestly to get out of the monastic tutelage in which they vegetate, neither would the friars rule the Philippines *nor modern ideas be asphyxiated upon touching the shores of Manila* (emphasis mine). (ibid., 289)

Rizal's growing pro-independence stance solidified amid a belief that Spanish governance, even in its most liberal guise, would continue to produce injustices in the colony. It was therefore the task of Filipino liberals to take their country's fate into their own hands, and promote "modern ideas" themselves. Rizal could be vague about what it meant to claim the mantle of liberalism. At times, he simply meant that Filipino liberals should lead the parliamentary lobby in Europe. At other times, he discussed a peaceful evolution to independence with Filipino intellectuals leading gradual change. At times, he alluded to revolution. But in all these cases, Rizal was consistent on the need for sacrifice.

Rizal believed that pain would make Filipinos worthy of liberty's gifts. Writing to members of the La Solidaridad Association, he declared that "Liberty is a woman who grants her favors only to the brave. Enslaved peoples have to suffer much to win her and those who abuse her lose her. Liberty is not obtained *bobilis bobilis*, (without pain or merit) nor is it granted *gratis et amore*" (Reformists, 314). If taken for granted, liberty slips away. Those who sought it required a tough patriotism that would allow them to sacrifice for the liberal nation.

Pain was necessary for liberals to prove themselves. But the pain they suffered would also embolden more liberals to emerge. "Our enemies will be terrified upon encountering a youth that fears nothing when it comes to serving his country, a youth that is not deterred by the vengeance currently practiced," he wrote to Ponce in 1889. "What I said will be fulfilled, that *the more vexations are committed the more Filipino liberals will emerge* (emphasis mine)" (Reformists, 352). The pain of the liberal therefore serves as the light that will allow new liberals to see the world more clearly. Those who suffer have access to a distinct epistemology, since they have firsthand experience of oppression, which clarifies one's political vision.

Rizal's concern for a purified liberalism may explain his fixation with martyrdom, typified in a comment from 1890, where he claimed that "We die only once and of we do not die well, we lose a good opportunity which will never come up again" (Reformists, 479). Martyrdom was not only proof of the suffering necessary for the birth of liberty; it was also proof of "vexations committed" that would inspire more liberals to emerge. Rizal understood the power of martyrdom because he himself had become a liberal nationalist through the example of the martyred Fr. Burgos. As early as June 1892, on his way home to the Philippines from Hong Kong and more than four years before his actual execution, Rizal had already anticipated his death, and viewed it as part of a struggle for national redemption. In a letter to the Filipino people which he asked to be published after his death, he wrote:

> I have always loved my poor country and I am sure that I shall love her until death if by chance men are unjust to me; and I shall enjoy the happy life, contended in the thought that all that I have suffered, my past, my present and my future, my life, my loves, my pleasures, I have sacrificed for her. Happen what may, I shall die blessing her and desiring the dawn of her redemption. (PHW, 333)

The theme of sanctification through suffering is no doubt a Christian one, and it was the Christian undertones of Rizal's martyrdom that made his death resonate among millenarian sects (there are groups who, until today, view Rizal as a Tagalog Christ). But Rizal's belief in suffering as a prerequisite for liberty is neither utopian nor millenarian; it does not envision a revolutionary break that will change society overnight. Rather, small sacrifices, in response to multiple "vexations," engender a culture of liberalism and embolden liberals to take stances and make sacrifices. This process is gradual, as various citizens debate and construct national values.

Revolutionary Breaks

How would a liberal movement born from pain and suffering emerge? What would it look like? It is difficult to ascertain what steps Rizal saw as necessary for the creation of a liberal nation. Rizal was not programmatic, and he never wrote anything akin to Lenin's "What Must Be Done." Moreover, he wrote at a time of great censorship and repression in the Philippines. What he said could compromise not only his safety but that of his family. For while Rizal wrote in the security of Europe, his parents and siblings were all in the Philippines, subject to the whims of the friars and the colonial government. Despite his lack of a concrete vision for a liberal project, we may glean some insights on Rizal's views on liberal movements by looking at how he viewed other liberal movements and revolutions of the period.

Among Asian nations, the Philippines is unique in that its nationalist movement blossomed at a time before the mainstreaming of Marxism in general and Leninist Communism in particular. Rizal's twentieth-century counterparts like Ho Chi Minh could look to the Russian and Chinese revolutions as inspirations. But Rizal's generation could only draw from liberal revolutions.[1] They would have been inspired by these examples, but they would have also been aware of the pattern of counter-revolution and terror triggered by these events.

It is thus unfair for contemporary historians to dismiss Rizal as not radical enough (see Rafael 2015) simply because he was a liberal and because he was cautious about revolutionary violence. We must place him in his Victorian context—a context where liberal radicals vigorously debated the legacies of violent revolt. Rizal admired the French Revolution and likewise admired its American counterpart. But he was also aware of Jacobin Terror, and he would have known about the carnage that followed the Paris Commune years later. Rizal was not one to advocate violence simply because it was the more drastic option. Rather, he asked under what conditions a revolution would lead to a liberal republic.

Although Rizal visited and wrote about many countries, his thoughts on the United States shed light on his views on liberal revolution. Few contemporary historians realize that, in one of the few times Rizal considered what a Philippine revolution in Spain might look like, he cited the US example favorably.

Rizal visited America from April to May 1888, where he visited San Francisco, Sacramento, Salt Lake City, Chicago, and New York (Ocampo

---

[1] Like Conrad, Rizal could, of course, also reference the anarchist bombings of the period. However, as with Conrad as well, Rizal's allusions to anarchy were more literary devices and ethical heuristics rather than hints at a political program.

2012, 17). In certain ways, notes Ocampo (ibid., 20), "Rizal was a European in spirit and felt slighted by the unfair comparisons between Europe and America." And he likewise felt a disdain for what he viewed as the parochialism of the Americans he encountered in his various voyages.

He nevertheless felt a deep admiration for the United States as a bastion of liberal freedoms. He believed that the American revolutionaries fought a "just cause" that could be replicated by Filipinos should peaceful means be exhausted (Reformists, 353), and revered Washington as "the great man whom I believe has no second in this century (ibid., 187)." Again, these ideas would not have made him any different from many European liberals at the time. For, although many of them disdained the crassness of the New World, they would have also been inspired by the launching of liberal republican experiment across the Atlantic.

Despite an awareness of America's original sin of slavery, Rizal remained naïve about the United States. In one of his flights of fancy, Rizal envisioned the future of the Philippines after Spain. He did not think that other European countries would try to colonize the country after Spain's failure. The European powers in Asia already had enough on their plates. He noted, however, that:

> Perhaps the great American Republic, whose interests lie in the Pacific and which has no share in the spoils of Africa, may one day think of overseas possessions. It is not impossible for a bad example is catching, covetousness and ambition are the vices of the powerful ... but the European powers could not give her a free hand for they well know that appetite grows first with morsels; North America would be too awkward a rival if someday she took up the practice. Anyway it would be against her traditions. (Quoted in Guerrero 2012, 244)

Guerrero (2012, 244) saw this statement as a "mistake made in good faith, out of idealism." Unfortunately for Rizal, the United States would "find her traditions inconvenient" (ibid.), for it would indeed colonize the Philippines after Spain.

Whatever we may say about the flaws in Rizal's assessment of the United States, his thoughts on the American Revolution show that Rizal did entertain the possibility of liberal revolution. The question of under what conditions Rizal would have endorsed a liberal revolution, however, has been subject to vigorous debate.

REVOLUTION AND VIOLENCE

Rizal was both romantic and a realist. On the one hand, his position on martyrdom for his *patria* exemplifies the romanticism of any nationalist movement. On the other hand, he had no illusions about singular acts and events being enough to earn a people liberty. Perhaps a revolution may lead to independence, but not necessarily the creation of a national community founded on liberal values. He viewed the creation of a liberal polity as a long-term endeavor, produced by a nation that was capable of defending their rights and those of others. "A people," he explained in a statement for his 1896 trial, "can be free without being independent, and a people can be independent without being free" (PHW, 340). For him, "liberties" were more important than political independence (ibid.).

One of the biggest debates about Rizal's legacy is whether or not he supported the Philippine Revolution of 1896. It was axiomatic in twentieth-century Philippine historiography that Rizal was a bourgeois "moderate," who condemned what Teodoro Agoncillo (1956) falsely labeled *The Revolt of the Masses*. Recent revisionist history, however, has shown that, though Rizal doubted the military capacity of the rebels to launch a successful revolution, he admired their intentions (Quibuyen 1997). And as early as the 1960s, Guerrero (2012, 332) had already shown that the Katipunan may have been an offshoot of the organizing Rizal did for *La Liga Filipina*.

In his defense statement during his trial, Rizal equivocated (which probably contributed to his conviction), denying his involvement with revolution but holding out on the belief "that if Spain systematically denied liberties to the Philippines, there would be insurrections" (PHW, 340). Taken in the context of Rizal's other writings, this statement is telling, because his works, especially his novels (see next chapter), were sustained arguments about the impossibility of liberal reform under a system of friar dominance. Even while defending himself, he could not help but admit that "rebellious and punishable ideas have crossed my imagination, especially when my family was being persecuted, but afterwards reflection, the reality of facts, the absurdity of the thought, made me recover my senses, because I don't believe I'm stupid or foolish to want an impossible and senseless thing" (PHW, 346).

The picture of a reformist Rizal is further complicated if we examine a document written *after* his trial and conviction. As Floro Quibuyen (1997,

244) points out, the "last word" on Rizal's take on the revolution should be his untitled last poem (now called *Mi Ultimo Adios* (My Final Farewell)), which his sister smuggled out of his cell and gave to the revolutionaries. While the defense statement was written by a man on trial, the final poem was written by someone who had already accepted his fate. There is some controversy concerning the poem's translation (see ibid., 244–245), so I will use the original Spanish, and provide a literal, if unpoetic, translation. In the second stanza Rizal notes:

> *En campos de batalla, luchando con delirio*
> *Otros te dan sus vidas sin dudas, sin pesar*
> *El sitio nada importa, ciprés, laurel o lirio*
> *Cadalso o campo abierto, combate o cruel martirio*
> *Lo mismo es si lo piden la Patria y el Hogar*

> (On fields of battle, fighting with delirium
> Others give you their lives without doubts, without regret
> The place does not matter, cypress, laurel or lily
> Scaffold or open field, combat or cruel martyrdom
> The same is true if asked for by the Country and the Home)

Here, Rizal equates his death with those of fallen revolutionaries, celebrating their martyrdom for the nation. It is not a direct endorsement of the Katipunan's revolution, as Quibuyen thinks. Rather, it signifies an openness to revolutionary violence given the right conditions. At best, we can speculate that Rizal admired the revolutionaries and shared their belief that reform was hopeless under the Spanish government. But we must also acknowledge his lingering ambivalence about revolutionary violence and the immediate creation of a new political system without adequate preparation. Add to this his perennial concern about the military viability of the Katipunan's revolt. We shall explore further in Chap. 4 why Rizal was more concerned with the long-term goal of cultivating liberties than the short-term goal of independence.

Conclusion

Rizal was without a doubt a nineteenth-century liberal, focused on key rights such as the freedom of religion, freedom of the press, and beneficent economic governance from above. His rights-based liberalism drew on Enlightenment beliefs about broad principles shared by humanity. He was a universalist, but his concerns were also local. No European could understand the travails of a liberal in the colony, because for Rizal, Europeans did not suffer as colonials did. They may have suffered under fellow compatriots like reactionary kings whom they could increasingly challenge in the nineteenth century. But they were never forced to conform to an external power that made them follow rules created by faceless bodies from thousands of miles away.

The idea that the denial of liberty is more pronounced and acute in colonial contexts is, naturally, applicable to present postcolonies. Poverty and injustice are more pressing in the present-day Global South. In many ways, however, Rizal was a product of the times. Thus, while he was cognizant of racial difference, present-day liberals would find his thoughts on class and gender wanting.

Like most liberals of this period, Rizal's concern for universality eclipsed his capacity to see various forms of marginality. The popular perception of Rizal was that he was "a bourgeois idealist" who put "his faith in reason and liberal dogmas of the inevitability of progress, like any proper Victorian, and preferring reform to revolution, and 'revolution from above' to 'revolution from below'" (Joaquin 2005, 52). Although Rizal's novels feature multiple downtrodden characters—some of whom even organize to form rebellious groups to challenge the avariciousness of friars or the authoritarianism of the civil guards—Rizal does not imbue them with a political program that hints at wealth redistribution. In the *Noli*, the budding revolutionaries merely seek justice amid the arbitrary application of the criminal justice system.

As for gender, Rizal and the propagandists often portrayed friars as overly sexualized and predatory toward Filipino women. But these ideas were more informed by a disdain for friar hypocrisy than a concern for women's rights. Rizal did write a famous letter to women in the province of Malolos who demanded for education in Castillan (PHW, 56–66), and this, indeed, hints at an early feminism. Yet Rizal's notion of rights were more anchored on universal liberties, with little acknowledgment of gender difference. And he never theorized the role of women as leaders in political movements.

In extolling Rizal's liberalism and arguing for its applicability today, I do not wish to deny the real blind spots of his vision. As liberalism grows, it improves and it recognizes more hindrances to human freedom. For his time, however, Rizal wrote eloquently about a unique vision of liberty that resonated with many of his compatriots, who, like him, experienced the suffering of a colonized people. And nowhere was this incendiary vision more evident than in his two novels.

BIBLIOGRAPHY

Agoncillo, Teodoro A. 1956. *The Revolt of the Masses.* Quezon City: University of the Philippines.

Evans, Richard J. 2016. *The Pursuit of Power.* New York: Viking.

Gray, John. 2000. *Two Faces of Liberalism.* New York: The New Press.

Guerrero, Leon Ma. 2012. *The First Filipino: A Biography of Jose Rizal.* Makati City: Guerrero Publishing.

———. 2013. Rizal as Liberal; Bonifacio and Democrat. In *Pens as Swords: The Philippine PEN Jose Rizal Lectures, 1958–2007,* ed. Jose Victor Torres. Manila: Solidaridad Publishing House.

Hobsbawm, Eric J. 1989. *The Age of Empire, 1875–1914.* New York: Vintage Books.

———. 1996. *The Age of Revolution: 1789–1848.* New York: Vintage.

———. 1997. *The Age of Capital, 1848–1875.* London: Abacus.

Joaquin, Nick. 2005. *A Question of Heroes.* Pasig City: Anvil Publishing Inc.

Mehta, Uday Singh. 1999. *Liberalism and Empire.* Chicago/London: University of Chicago Press.

Ocampo, Ambeth R. 2012. *Rizal Without the Overcoat.* Pasig City: Anvil Publishing Inc.

Perry, Martin, et al. 2009. *Western Civilization: Ideas, Politics, and Society.* 9th ed. Boston/New York: Houghton Mifflin Harcourt Publishing Company.

Polasky, Janet. 2015. *Revolutions Without Borders: The Call to Liberty in the Atlantic World.* New Haven: Yale University Press.

Quibuyen, Floro. 1997. Rizal and the Revolution. *Philippine Studies: Historical and Ethnographic Viewpoints* 45 (2): 225–257.

Rafael, Vicente L. 2015. Introduction: Revolutionary Contradictions. In *Luzon at War: Contradictions in Philippine Society, 1898–1902,* ed. Milagros Camayon Guerrero, 1–19. Mandaluyong City: Anvil Publishing Inc.

Schumacher, John N. 1997. *The Propaganda Movement: 1880–1895: The Creation of a Filipino Consciousness, the Making of a Revolution.* Quezon City: Ateneo de Manila University Press.

Thomas, Megan C. 2012. *Orientalists, Propagandists, and Ilustrados: Filipino Scholarship and the End of Spanish Colonialism.* Minneapolis/London: University of Minnesota Press.

CHAPTER 3

Noli me Tangere and the Failure of Transplanted Liberalism

Abstract This chapter is an introduction to and a liberal interpretation of Rizal's first novel, *Noli Me Tangere*. It provides an overview of Rizal as a novelist, explains Rizal's notion of audience, and moves to a discussion of the *Noli*'s themes. In the novel, Rizal uses the skills of a journalist to reproduce nineteenth-century Philippine society with fidelity. He then uses this setting to test the viability of liberal reformism in the country. The novel's main character, the creole/mestizo Juan Crisostomo Ibarra, tries to build a progressive school in the European mold. For his efforts, the friars brand him a subversive and frame him for inciting rebellion. Ibarra's failure stems not only from his naiveté but also from his misunderstanding of how liberalism should be cultivated in the colony.

Keywords *Noli me Tangere* • Liberalism • Rizal • Nationalism • Novel

The novels of Rizal, writes Caroline Hau (2000, 48), are the "'originary,' if not founding, fictions of the Filipino national community." They are also, she adds, assertions of the national community's modernity—"attempts at describing a historical context in which the nation form had already achieved normative status in other places as the principal mode of social organization and political imagination" (ibid., 52).

© The Author(s) 2019   37
L. E. Claudio, *Jose Rizal*, Global Political Thinkers,
https://doi.org/10.1007/978-3-030-01316-5_3

What were the contours of this nation? And what was the modernity that Rizal's novels sought to promote? In this chapter, I contend that Rizal's concept of modernity was linked to his project of liberalism in the colony. Both his novels interrogate existing models of liberalism in the hope of letting readers define a new version for their nation. Although they are intentionally open-ended and invite constant interpretation, they are circumscribed by the universal liberal principles that Rizal voiced in his essays and letters.

Contemporary scholars ignore the explicit liberalism in Rizal's novels. This is especially the case in leftwing North American literary studies, where the term "radical" is the academic equivalent of "good guy," and "liberal moderate" that of "bad guy." A recent study of the novels by Aaron C. Castroverde (2013, 178), for example, concludes that Rizal's work is a "takedown of the Spanish liberal project," which proved that "Rizal was much more radical than his Spanish contemporaries." Castroverde is no doubt correct to argue that Rizal was more radical than the Spaniards he criticized. But he fails to outline the contours of Rizal's radicalism. Rizal was, indeed, radical, but he remained a liberal in disposition and orientation, because, as we noted earlier, liberalism in the nineteenth century was radical.

Rizal's works may have been critiques of Spanish liberalism as practiced, but, as we saw in the previous chapter, this critique did not mean a rejection of liberalism writ large. If alternative political programs may be found in Rizal's novels, these remain anchored on his idea of a liberalism purified through pain. The liberal spirit of his novels can be gleaned from not just their content but also the reactions of Rizal's peers. In 1891, for example, the painter Juan Luna claimed that Rizal was the "creator" of the Philippine novel, who would "establish with his writings freedom of thought, which is the foremost liberty, if not the only one that man possesses" (Reformists, 599). For Luna, Rizal's novels were treatises on the rights of man.

Rizal and his peers knew that their creative works dovetailed with the forging an Enlightenment inspired by liberal creed. Such is evident not only in Rizal's novels, but in Luna's own paintings, in particular his *Spoliarium*, which depicts dead gladiators being dragged off an arena. Rizal referred to the painting as representing an "unredeemed mankind," where "reason and aspiration" are in an "open struggle with "preoccupations, fanaticism, and injustices" (PHW, 20). Rizal wanted his novels to do for literature what Luna' did for visual art. He wanted to show that Filipinos could, like Europeans, promote Enlightenment through their work.

But the advocacy for Enlightenment would not simply consist of moral exhortations. Something was rotten in the Philippines, and Rizal wanted to expose it. Only through literary muckraking could he unearth the barriers toward progress—barriers not just erected by reactionary friars, but by failed liberals unable to adhere to their principles in the Philippines. If liberalism were to flourish in the colony, it had to be fused with a selfless patriotism that allowed liberals to purify their intentions. The liberalism of the *Noli* was therefore not only a struggle against society's reactionaries, but also an interior struggle with one's self.

RIZAL'S MULTIPLE AUDIENCES

Rizal's brother, Paciano, emphasized that Rizal went to Europe for a more noble purpose than just obtaining professional credentials. He was there for the nationalist cause, and written propaganda was his immediate priority. In 1884, Rizal proposed to his fellow expatriates that they write a collective book on various aspects of Philippine life and culture (Guerrero 2012, 130). Its goal would be to introduce Filipinos to Europeans, who knew nothing about the colony. Guerrero (2012, 130) explains that Rizal wanted to show that "they were not naked savages brandishing tomahawks," but were instead "Oriental Europeans." Nothing became of the project.

The idea of writing a novel percolated shortly after. Rizal had been impressed by how his colleagues, the painters Juan Luna and Felix Resurrection Hidalgo, mastered the salon painting of European masters, celebrating their victories in artistic competitions as proof of the Filipino's rightful place in European modernity. Rizal sought to win similar recognition through the novel, hoping to write in the tradition of European realist masters like Hugo, Zola, Daudet, and Dickens (ibid., 131). In particular, he was inspired by Eugene Sue's anti-clerical novel, *The Wandering Jew* (Schumacher 1997, 91).[1] He would begin work on his first novel, *Noli me Tangere*, shortly after abandoning the collective book project. When he departed for Paris from Madrid in the middle of 1895, he had completed half of the work, finishing the rest in Germany, where the book would also be printed in March 1887 (ibid., 22).

[1] Based on the books that Rizal left with Jose Ma. Basa in Hong Kong, we know that his library contained many French titles: works by Honore de Balzac, Alexander Dumas, Pierre Jean de Beranger, Moliere, Charles de Secondat Montesquieu, and Emile Zola (Ocampo 2012, 75).

While the *Noli* is not nationalist in the narrow sense of advocating separation from Spain (Rizal was not yet an advocate of independence at this point), it is nationalist in its vista, because it envisioned a knowable national community. As Benedict Anderson notes (1998, 230), the space of the novel is definite, and although there are multiple characters—many of them from Spain—their Spain "is always off stage." "The restriction," he concludes, "made it clear to Rizal's first readers that 'The Philippines' was a society in itself, even though those who lived in it had as yet no common name." Hau (2017, 156) adds that the novel imagines a national community because of its constant references to crowds, gathering for multiple purposes, creating a sense of the public. These crowds are not just spectators, but active participants and commentators, integral to the novel's plot.

Though the *Noli* was not the first novel authored by a Filipino,[2] it was the first novel set in a definite national imagination, written for a national community. The writing of the *Noli* occurred as Rizal was beginning to rethink questions of audience, amid a growing concern for the formation of a Philippine national literature—a move away from the ilustrado artistic practice of seeking recognition within Europe. The works of early propaganda movement in Spain were mostly addressed to foreigners, and the increasing refinement of the ilustrados' style proved their capacity to address European intellectuals. The publication of the *Noli*, however, marked a shift toward nationalists addressing their own compatriots and viewing them as part of a new community.

The resolution to speak to one's countrymen was not without tension. Despite his goal to speak to Filipinos in the Philippines, Rizal still wrote in Europe, alongside companions who were lobbying for assimilation in Europe. Historian Resil B. Mojares (2013, 216) explains the ambivalence of this position:

> On the one hand, they were claiming, for Filipinos, a personality and visibility within the empire, as an autonomous province or region in an idealized federal republic—like Galicia or Catalonia in the peninsula or, overseas, Cuba and Puerto Rico. When they extolled their Malay heritage, the richness of local languages and literature, it was to seek recognition as an equal, if distant member of Greater Spain. On the other hand, they were resisting assimilation into Spanish-imperial literary space that would ignore or erase difference, by staking out the cultural autonomy of a nation that could, if events dictate, become a separate nation-state.

[2] That honor belongs to the 1885 novel *Ninay*, written by Pedro Paterno.

It is this ambivalence that likely explains why Rizal's novels were written in Spanish, and not Tagalog.[3] For, although they were nationalist works, they were still conscious attempts to locate the Philippines within the modernity represented by Europe. Still, the *Noli* was a departure from Rizal's original plan of writing a primer on Filipinos for Europeans. It was an explicit attempt to address his countrymen directly, in a provocative style aimed to spur political action. In letters to his fellow propagandists, Rizal was clear about his intended audience: The *Noli* was "written for Filipinos" and "should be read by Filipinos." It was written "for my country" and to "arouse the feelings of my countrymen" (Quoted in Guerrero 2012, 149).

The novel itself rehashes this intent in a dedication called "To My Country." The dedication opens with a medical metaphor, noting that, in comparing his country to others, its "beloved image" appeared to him as a "social cancer." Desiring the country's "good health," "I will do with you what the ancients did with their infirmed: they placed them on the steps of their temples so that each in his own way could invoke a divinity that might offer a cure" (*Noli*, 3).[4] One could almost say, in contemporary parlance, that Rizal was crowdsourcing a solution to the country's problems. His job as author would be to "reproduce your current conditions faithfully, without prejudice," while that of the reader would be to help find a remedy (ibid.).

Because of the novel's avowed goal seeking a collective memory to the country's social cancer, there are no concrete proposals for change in the novel. It does not, for example, address the question of independence. Neither does the novel take a definitive position on revolution, despite the revolutions in Spain's American colonies.

Despite these vagaries, the novel was immediately branded subversive in the Philippines. Without approval from the official censors, it had to be smuggled into the country in June 1887 (Schumacher 1997, 92). As the

---

[3] One must also consider the possibility that Rizal, who acknowledged the ethno-linguistic diversity of the Philippines, was ambivalent about such outright assertions of Tagalog supremacy. See Ocampo (2012, 5–8) for an account of how a poem falsely attributed to Rizal has been used to promote Tagalog language supremacy.

[4] Hau (2017, 164) has recently shown that Rizal's metaphor mixes two ancient practices. The Greeks spent the night in front of the temple, hoping for the gods or the priests to discover a remedy. The Babylonians, on the other hand, may have placed sick people in public squares, hoping for passersby to suggest cures.

books started circulating, a report from the Dominican-run University of Santo Tomas declared that it was "heretical, impious and scandalous in the religious order, and antipatriotic, subversive of public order, offensive to the government of Spain and to its method of procedure in these Islands in the political order" (quoted in ibid., 93). After significant censure and intense lobbying from friars, the colonial government arrested and jailed those found in possession of the book (ibid., 102).

Rizal was visiting the Philippines shortly after the *Noli*'s publication, and he was forced to leave because of the controversy it generated. "My family would not allow me to eat in any house, for fear that they might poison me," he narrated in 1888. To give his family peace, he returned to Europe, with many Filipinos believing that he was "lucky to have escaped unharmed from the Philippines" (Misc. letters, 99). Rizal quoted Schiller to describe his feelings: "I have seen horrible things, monsters which menaced me with their talons; but by the help of God I am again on the surface." Amid the "free air of Europe," Rizal would be able to continue his propaganda work (ibid.).

Rizal's earliest biographer, Wenceslao Retana (1907, 139), notes an irony in these events. Rizal's return should have been joyful, for both Spain and the Philippines at the time were under liberal rule. But the friars exerted too much influence on even the most liberal officials, leading to the suppression of Rizal's work. Rizal should not have been surprised, since what happened to him happens to his novel's protagonist. As we shall see, Crisostomo Ibarra, though friendly with the liberal governor general, is unable to escape friar persecution.

The novel was controversial, but it would not have been read by a large audience. It was written in Spanish, and literacy in this language was at roughly 2% of the population in the late nineteenth century (Abinales and Amoroso 2017, 95). Moreover, its eventual banning further limited its circulation. Hence the novel's influence spread not through direct reading, but rumor. As Hau (2000, 55) argues, state censorship "made possible the production of a specific form of reading that sidestepped proscription but permitted, nevertheless, a relaying of the novel's content." It is also likely that the scorn from the friars made people aware of a writer brave enough to court the ire of the country's colonial masters. The *Noli* made Rizal famous. And all succeeding controversies and accusations related to him would center on his reputation as the author of incendiary literature.

THE LIBERAL EXPERIMENT IN *NOLI*

If Rizal took pains to reconstruct his country, it was because his goals were empirical. One can read both Rizal's novels as twin experiments in two kinds of change, both associated with variants of liberalism. The *Noli* represents the Philippines of the nineteenth century so that Rizal may use its main character, the creole/mestizo Juan Crisostomo Ibarra, to test the viability of liberal reformism in the country. On the other hand, the *Fili* was an experiment in Jacobin revolution. The realism of the novels allowed Rizal to assess political programs within a veritable Philippines of the late nineteenth century.

True events form the backdrop of the *Noli*: the Spanish Glorious Revolution of 1868, the opening of the Suez in 1869, La Torre's liberal administration of the Philippines (1869–1871), and the execution of Burgos, Gomez, and Zamora in 1872 (Mojares 1983, 144). There are, however, no overseas propagandists in this version of the Philippines, and Rizal places him and his colleagues outside the temporal and geographic reach of the novel. It is a time after the repression of 1872, but we are unsure if it covers the period of overseas agitation. We can, however, place the timeline of the novel at 1883 or earlier, because, in one scene, the character Elias claims that it is almost 15 years since the institution of the Civil Guard (ibid., 321), which was 1868.[5]

The *Noli*'s plot begins when the idealistic Ibarra returns to the Philippines after seven years of study in Europe. Ibarra is wealthy, from a family of Basque ancestry known for its beneficence, and he is described as an "amiable Rothschild of the Philippines" (*Noli*, 187). A Manila front-page article calls him an "illustrious young man and wealthy capitalist" and a "distinguished philanthropist," a "student of Minerva who had gone to the mother country to pay homage to the true origin of the arts and science" (ibid., 178).

He arrives eager to promote the ideals of his deceased father—a prominent creole from the town of San Diego (loosely modeled on Rizal's hometown of Calamba)—of educational reform and to reunite with his betrothed, Maria Clara. Ibarra himself is a mestizo, the son of a creole father and the

---

[5] The phrasing of the line precludes exact dating. Elias says that it will be 15 years "pronto." *Pronto* could mean a few days, a few weeks, a few months, or even a few years. Whatever the case, we can be sure that the *Noli* occurred in the past, since 1887, the date of the novel's publication, is after 15 years from the foundation of the Civil Guard. I thank Carol Hau for the back-and-forth email discussion on the dating of *Noli me Tangere*.

native mother.[6] But since creolism in the Philippines referred more to one's politics and not race, Ibarra must be read as a creole, representing the liberal politics of thinkers like Varela, whom we discussed in Chap. 1.

The first chapter sees Ibarra at a dinner in the house of Maria Clara's father, Don Santiago de los Santos, or "Captain Tiago." Here, he remeets Father Damaso, a Franciscan who was San Diego's curate when he left for Europe. To Ibarra's surprise, Damaso, whom he recalled as dear friend of his deceased father, is cold, even hostile, to him.

Ibarra discovers through a Spanish solider that his father, the wealthiest man in the town, had an unexplained falling out with the Franciscan. When the older Ibarra accidentally killed a Spanish tax collector, the authorities sent him to jail, where he would be left to die. Because he was a freethinker and refused to go to confession, Damaso denied Ibarra's father a Christian burial. He was initially interred in a Chinese cemetery. But Ibarra discovers from a gravedigger that the body was exhumed and thrown into the sea.

Believing himself a forgiving Catholic and loyal subject of Spain, Ibarra seeks to honor the memory of his father not through revenge, but through philanthropy. For much of the first half of the novel, he attempts to build a modern school for his town. Such an institution, modeled after the schools Ibarra had seen in Germany, would provide an alternative to friar-dominated education, which taught barely more than rote catechism.[7]

If the *Noli* is an experiment in liberal reformism, its testing ground— the independent variable—is the Philippines. And the dependent variable is the school, an undertaking that, according to Hau (2004, 154), Ibarra views as "a rational application of the European enlightenment principle of education and empowerment through the cultivation of young people's moral and intellectual capacities." Ibarra's faith in progress and enlightenment were bound up with the project. It was a faith premised on not only his reformism but also his dedication to the memory of his deceased father.

At the laying of the school's cornerstone, the scaffolding collapses, and Ibarra barely escapes death. Elias, a mysterious boatman whose life Ibarra had saved (Chap. 4), pushes Ibarra away from the falling stones. Though the narrator is uncertain, he hints that the "accident" may have been the

---

[6] His middle name is the Magsalin—a Tagalog word for pouring into another receptacle. It also means to translate.

[7] It is partly the novel's admiration for German education that gave critics ammunition to describe the novel as "protestant" and "unpatriotic" to Spain.

work of the Franciscan Father Salvi, the new parish priest who secretly covets Maria Clara. The assassination attempt is the first indication that Ibarra's plans will end in tragedy.

A parallel conflict between Ibarra and Father Damaso imperils the young man's plan to wed Maria Clara. At a banquet during the town fiesta, Damaso continues his diatribes against Ibarra, who does his best to bite his tongue. But when the friar insults the memory of his dead father, Ibarra knocks the friar to the ground. Before Ibarra is able to deal a lethal blow, Maria Clara intervenes.

The altercation gives the friars a reason to excommunicate Ibarra, which imperils his relationship with Maria Clara. Captain Tiago, succumbing to pressure, forbids his daughter and Ibarra from seeing each other again. In turn, Father Damaso, whom the reader will eventually discover to be Maria Clara's biological father, arranges a new marriage between Maria Clara and a peninsular relative named Linares.

Meanwhile, a group of villagers—people who have been abused by the Civil Guard or denied justice in courts—are organizing an uprising. Elias, who is close to the rebels, convinces them that, instead of an insurrection, they should first seek the support of Ibarra, who could serve as the spokesman of the downtrodden. But when Elias proposes this role to Ibarra, the latter refuses. Ibarra continues to focus on his school, while rebellion brews.

The experiment in reform that the novel rehearses is a complete failure. The novel's denouement, explains Schumacher (1997, 85), occurs when "all those who have expressed liberal opinions or who have offended the friar are imprisoned, chief among them Ibarra." Salvi frames the protagonist for fomenting revolution through a distorted interpretation of letters sent to Maria Clara. After being sent to jail, Ibarra escapes with the aid of Elias, who smuggles him away through the river Pasig.

Bereft of public and personal glory, Ibarra turns insurrectionary. Explaining that "misfortune has ripped off my blinders," he claims to "see the horrible cancer gnawing at this society, rotting its flesh, almost begging for a violent extirpation." Hence he would not just "be a subversive, but a true subversive," one who would "call together all the downtrodden people, everyone who feels a heart beating in his breast (*Noli*, 400)."

The novel ends with a final tragedy: the death of its most noble character, Elias. During the escape, the authorities shoot Elias, believing him to be Ibarra. Ridden with gunshot wounds, Elias dies in the forest of the vast Ibarra property. With the authorities believing him dead, Ibarra escapes the Philippines.

FAILED EXPERIMENT

Why does Ibarra's attempt at liberal reformism fail? Throughout the novel, Rizal is scornful of the naiveté and selfishness of his main character. Although Filipino school children are raised to believe that the reformist Ibarra is a stand-in for a likewise reformist author,[8] it is clear that Rizal's views are not those of Ibarra's. "I am neither rich nor *mestizo*, nor an orphan, nor do the qualities of Ibarra coincide with mine," he told Vicente Barrantes, a member of the Real Academia de Lengua (PHW, 187). In a conversation with Jose Alejandrino, an eventual general in the Philippine revolution, he also explained that he was fonder of Elias than Ibarra. The former was "a noble character, patriotic, self-denying and disinterested," while the latter "was an egoist who only decided to provoke the rebellion when he was hurt in his interests, his person, his loves and all the other things he held sacred" (Quoted in Quibuyen 1997, 229).

Ibarra's patriotism, as Hau (2004, 164) explains, is "married to personal happiness because it derives its original inspiration from his filial love for his father, from the wellspring of happy memories of youth, and from his desire for Maria Clara." So he becomes focused on his personal affairs, distracted from his reformist goals and "blind to the unmistakable signs of discontent and plotting around him" (ibid., 163). Similarly, literary critic Petronilo Daroy (1968, 91) notes that Ibarra's "sense of responsibility is only indirectly social; foremost in his mind is the idea of clan."

Ibarra is oblivious to the dark clouds in the distance. He believes that his project is simple, and uncontroversial. But, as Rafael Palma (1949, 79), explains, Ibarra did not understand his own country, noting that "In any country a project to build a school would have been supported by all; in the Philippines, however, things happened differently."[9] Palma, like many critics, claims that the *Noli*'s power lies in its realism, its accurate representation of the country and the attitudes of its people (ibid.). There are, therefore, no fantasies in the novel's pages. What catches up with Ibarra's liberal fantasy is the reality of reaction in the colony.

The novel foreshadows Ibarra's failure at multiple points. During a picnic in a forest, Ibarra, Maria Clara, and a group of friends pose questions to a Wheel of Fortune. At one point, Ibarra asks "Will my new project turn out well?" To which he receives the reply "Dreams are Dreams"

---

[8] The 1998 blockbuster-style film *Jose Rizal* (still the mostly widely seen cinematic biography of Rizal) asserts that Rizal gave Ibarra his eyes, so that they see the same things.

[9] Translation mine.

(*Noli*, 157). In the middle of the novel Elias warns Ibarra about a possible plot against him, saying "you need your enemies to think you are unprepared and trusting." Ibarra is puzzled and answers "My enemies? Do I have enemies?" (ibid., 219).

But the strongest warning comes from a village wiseman and scholar known as Tasio the Philosopher, whom "the impolite ones" called "Tasio the Madman because of his odd ideas and his strange manner of dealing with people" (ibid., 78). Since his late father often asked Tasio for counsel, Ibarra turned to him as well, and Ibarra's conversation with the old man explores how liberal ideas become lunacy in colonial Philippines.

Upon entering the philosopher's house, Ibarra discovers that the old man is writing hieroglyphics. Tasio says that he does not understand Egyptian or Coptic, but is merely using hieroglyphics to write in Tagalog, "So that no one will understand what I'm writing" (ibid., 162). He explains that he is "not writing for this generation," but "for the ages." Future generations would be more educated and would say "In the nights of our grandparents, not everyone was asleep" (ibid.). But for the present, his ideas were those of a madman.

Tasio advises Ibarra to "consult the priest, the mayor, and everyone in an important position." Though he would likely find their views useless, Ibarra should "Try to make it look as much as possible" as if he were "heeding their advice," making it clear that he is "working according to that advice." The image of working with authority was necessary, especially since the young man's return had wounded "the pride of a priest who the people believe is a saint and whose peers consider wise" (ibid., 165). "Here," adds Tasio, "if you don't bow your head, you will lose it" (ibid., 168).

Ibarra resists the counsel, reminding the older man "that among them they killed my father, and dragged him from his tomb...but I, his son, will not forget, and if I'm not taking revenge it's because I see religion's prestige" (ibid.).

Tasio replies that "if you hold on to those memories, memories I can't advise you to forget, abandon the task you have set before you and seek the welfare of the peasants in another arena. Such a task requires another man since, to bring it to fruition, it is only necessary to have money and desire, in our country one needs abnegation tenacity and faith, since the earth has not been tilled. It has to be sown only with discord" (ibid., 169).

Ibarra, however, "would not be dissuaded" as "The memory of Maria Clara remained in his mind. His offer had to succeed" (ibid.). Tasio concedes that some good may come out of the project, but only after certain catastrophe. "After the storm is unleashed, perhaps some grain will germinate, survive the catastrophe, save the species from annihilation and serve thereafter as the seed for the children to sow later" (ibid., 170). The germination of Ibarra's liberal plant would take some time, and would first have to die before being resurrected.

Ibarra halfheartedly accepts reality, understanding that, "with all his pessimism, the old man was right" (ibid., 170). Despite his concession, the chapter shows that our protagonist is driven more by pride than a concern for his country.

IBARRA AND HISTORICAL CREOLES

In creating an egotistical and naïve protagonist, Rizal was harkening back to his descriptions of earlier Filipino reformists whom he likewise viewed as selfish. Writing to Ponce, he noted that previous Filipinos, including Fr. Burgos whom he venerated, failed because of egoism (Reformists, 353). The work of future patriots, therefore, would be to elevate the nationalist movement to one anchored on sacrifice and selflessness.

Ibarra does not represent the Filipino liberal of the present or the future, but of the past. He is not an indio/native Filipino like Rizal, but a creole/mestizo like many of their forebears. And he symbolizes past liberal experiments of creoles in the Philippines—those of conducted by Varela and Burgos. The *Noli*, explains Joaquin (2005, 71), occurs in the epoch of these forebears and Ibarra "follows the fate of Burgos even to the point of being, like Burgos, implicated in an uprising he knows nothing about." Like Burgos, Ibarra proposes modest reform. And like Burgos, he is framed for advocating the most minimal changes.

The novel itself references the tragedy of 1872, and compares the multiple arrests that occurred amid Ibarra's framing to those that occurred after the Cavite Mutiny and Burgos's execution. The comparison is explicit in a conversation between Captain Tinong (a friend of Ibarra's fearing implication in the plot) and his wife, Captain Tinchang. In the scene, Tinchang tells Tinong that, because of her relationship with Ibarra "You have to go like they did in '72 to save themselves." "Sure," Tinong replies" that's what Father Burg—"But his wife does not allow him to finish, covering his mouth and shouting, "Stop! Say that name and tomorrow they'll hang you in Bagumbayan! Don't you know that simply by saying it you can be condemned without charges?" (ibid, 383).

The *Noli* is a requiem for the old politics of the creoles and early Filipino liberals. It is both a historical representation of these politics and a prediction about what would happen if nationalists reverted to simple reformism. As a diagnosis, the novel looks into not only the cancer of Philippine society but the failed ways in which reformists past have sought to treat it.

THE CONSCIENCE OF A LIBERAL

If Ibarra and his politics were not the solutions that Rizal sought, can we glean Rizal's true politics through other characters? We know from Alejandrino (see above) that Rizal respected Elias more than Ibarra. And there is certainly much to admire about the straggler who sacrifices his life for a flawed protagonist.[10] It is through Elias, explains Hau (2004, 162), that "Rizal offers his most fully realized elaboration of the disciplined, patriotic body." Unlike Ibarra, Elias gives up on romantic love and even family honor. For most of the novel, he lobbies for the poor and downtrodden, the *gente*, who may not benefit from the solutions Ibarra forwards. For Hau (2004, 162), Elias "challenges liberal assumptions concerning the 'rational' application of enlightenment principles to the 'ignorant' colonial populace." If there are shades of Ibarra in Rizal's own liberalism—as there definitely were despite Rizal's own distancing—he uses the character of Elias to challenge the limits of his beliefs.

Almost all of the characters in the *Noli*, explains Palma (1949, 81), are "sketches or portraits taken from real life." But Elias, because of his moral fortitude and the dramatic power of his story, is not "a model constructed from reality, but a pure allegorical creation."[11] It is through this allegorical character, borne from Rizal's ideal of self-sacrificing patriot, that the realities of the colony come into focus.

Elias is Ibarra's moral foil, and their debates mirror internal monologues Rizal must have rehearsed in the solitude of writing. In the final scene, Elias voices what are likely Rizal's own views about Ibarra's failings:

> You loved your country because your father taught you to do so, you loved it because you had love there, fortune, youth, because everything smiled down on you, because your country never did you any injustices, you loved

---

[10] During the height of the Marcos regime in the Philippines, Elias became a revolutionary symbol for many Maoist activists. My own parents, who were then members of the Communist Party, named me Lisandro Elias.

[11] Translation from Spanish mine.

it because we love anything that makes us happy. But on the day you find
yourself poor, hungry, persecuted, denounced, and sold out by your own
countrymen, on that day you will renounce yourself, your country, everything. (*Noli*, 400)

"Your words are painful," replies Ibarra. But Elias knew that pain was
necessary to "lift the scales" from Ibarra's eyes (ibid.). Elias hopes that the
wounds inflicted by the experience of loss and betrayal will change Ibarra.
For Elias, like Rizal, knows that pain purifies.

Rizal's moral exemplars are capable of sacrifice. We have seen how he
often complained about the selfish motivations of other patriots, but, in
Elias we see someone whose "sense of the patria is premised on (an already)
prior abdication of claims to love and personal happiness—in other words,
the claim to have a personal life at all—in favor of the higher claims of 'the
people'" (Hau 2004, 163–164). Elias saves Ibarra hoping that the latter
would discover new solutions to the country's ills, using his considerable
wealth to one day return and renew his campaign for progress. Not only
does Elias's death allow Ibarra to escape and return, it also allows for a
rebirth of his politics. Now aware of his country's rot, how its stink seeps
into every facet of colonial life, Ibarra is free to present a systematic alternative in the next novel.

PHILANTHROPY VERSUS ADVOCACY

Through Elias, Ibarra's moral failings become clear. Through Elias moreover, we discover the hypocrisies of Ibarra's liberalism. In a chapter titled
"Voice of the Persecuted," we learn the extent of Ibarra's myopia, when
Elias asks him to become the advocate of the bandits considering rebellion. "I am the bearer of the yearnings of many unhappy people," Elias
tells his friend (*Noli*, 319).

Elias declares that the persecuted seek "Radical reforms in the armed
forces, in the clergy, in the administration of justice, meaning they want
more paternal oversight on the government's part" (ibid., 320). He
explains that many poor people are subject to arbitrary arrests, failed trials,
and other miscarriages of justice, decrying the abuses committed by the
Civil Guard, which has "no more objective than the suppression of crime
by terror and force" (ibid.)

Ibarra pushes back, claiming that "Weakening the Civil Guard would
only endanger the people's security" (ibid., 321). Elias, stunned by the

reactionary stance of his interlocutor, argues that draconian measures have failed: "In the little while it will be fifteen years that these people have had the Civil Guard, and look: we still have bandits, we still hear about the sacking of villages, one is still accosted on the roads" (ibid., 321).[12] He then cites examples of routine abuses in various towns:

> They hone in on formalities and not the root of things, the first symptom of ineffectuality. When you forget your papers you have to be belittled and mistreated, no matter that the person is decent and respected. Officers believe that the most important responsibility is to be saluted according to their station or by force, even by dark of night, in which their inferiors imitate them and mistreat and fleece the peasants, on a variety of pretexts. There is no sanctity of one's home. A little while back in Calamba they stormed the house of a peaceful resident to whom their officer owed favors, coming in through the window. There is no individual security. When the barracks or a house needs cleaning, they go out and grab anyone who does not resist and make them work the whole day. (ibid., 322)

Elias is a budding revolutionary, but his concerns are those of a classical liberal: privacy and property rights ("sanctity of one's home"), the equal application of the law, and the regulation of unbridled state power. He is a liberal revolutionary, who envisions a society that upholds civil liberties. And, as the reader will soon find out, Elias's liberalism was purified through pain and suffering, because he and his family had experienced the capriciousness of justice in the colony. In his complex, melodramatic backstory, we learn that Elias was once wealthy, but the discovery that he was an illegitimate child of a prostitute's son forced him to renounce his fortune.[13] Since then, Elias has lived among those who suffer, shedding his privilege and sharing the pain of the *gente*.

---

[12] It is this same line that allows us to date the timeline of *Noli Me Tangere* to roughly 1883.

[13] His maternal grandfather, a bookkeeper, was framed for arson, which led to the family's penury. To raise their son (Elias's father), Elias's grandmother was forced into prostitution. Years later, Elias's father falls in love with a wealthy woman, and they have two children, Elias and his sister. But when his history is revealed, Elias's father goes to prison. Elias and his sister grow up believing that their father is dead. Their father, however, was a servant in their household—one they had mistreated multiple times. When Elias discovers his true identity, he abandons his wealth. The tragedy of this story becomes more pronounced when Elias discovers that it was Ibarra's great-grandfather who accused his grandfather of crime, thereby leading to the family's ruin.

As Elias narrates the abuses of the Civil Guard, Ibarra shocks him by claiming that "the government needs a body with unlimited power, so it will be respected and impose authority" (ibid., 323). Defending unrestricted state power, Ibarra's liberalism becomes compromised.

We find further proof of Ibarra's hypocrisy when the topic turns to the friars. Elias states that the friars have been "oppressors" of "unfortunate people," a statement which angers Ibarra. "Have Filipinos forgotten what they owe these orders?" he replies. "Have they forgotten the immense debt of gratitude they owe those who showed them the error of their ways and gave them faith, those who sheltered them from the tyranny of civilian power? This is the evil that comes from not teaching our country's history!" Elias, shocked, "could hardly believe his own ears" (ibid., 324). He comes to believe that he was wrong to invest so much faith in the young mestizo, lamenting that Ibarra ignorantly accuses "the people of ingratitude." "Allow me," he says, "one of the people who have suffered, to defend them" (ibid.).

It is against Elias's purified liberalism that Ibarra's is measured. Ibarra's liberal ideas are rooted in a desire to propagate his family's good name, while Elias discovered his commitment to liberal causes through his and other Filipino's suffering. Daroy (1968, 92) argues that because Ibarra's "actions do not contravene the sanctions of the *status quo*," that "His liberalism, as a consequence, jars against his personality, and renders his ideas contradictory." But it is not just that his liberalism contradicts his personality, it also that his liberalism is impure and ill-suited to the Philippines. Ibarra learned the value of liberty in the classrooms of Europe, amid relative openness and comfort. Earlier, Philosopher Tasio had detected that Ibarra was becoming "a plant transplanted from Europe to this rocky soil." "You are alone, highborn," he adds, "in terrible conditions" (*Noli*, 169).

In his arrogance, Ibarra tried to plant Spanish liberalism in his country. He did not realize that the soil required a new liberalism for the colony. He was naïve not only about the number of enemies he had. More importantly, he was naïve about the kind of liberal plant one needed to cultivate in the Philippines.

CONCLUSION

Despite its rejection of naïve reformism and its glorification of Elias, the *Noli* is not a program of action. Rizal took pains to argue that the *Noli* was not "anti-Catholic, Protestant, socialistic, and Proudhonian," as his critics had claimed (Letters to Blumentritt 1, 183). And in a letter to Ponce, he distanced himself from any of the injunctions of his characters, claiming that "the author is responsible only for the words that he says are his and the events and circumstances will justify the saying of the characters" (Reformists, 196). We do not therefore know which words Rizal holds himself accountable to, for even the *Noli*'s narrator is unreliable and inconsistent. Rizal keeps his audience guessing.

The novel's goal was simply to expose the colony's social cancer. The solutions would, as the dedication implied, come from the people collectively diagnosing the ills of the nation. Like a contemporary muckraking reporter, Rizal saw the expose as the first step. Despite his ambiguity about solutions, we already see in the *Noli* a number of key themes in Rizal's thinking that mirror those articulated in his essays and his letters. First, the *Noli* is a clear denunciation of the reactionary, friar-driven politics in the Philippines. Reading the *Noli* conjures a backward country, where ideas of enlightenment are "asphyxiated" before arriving at the shores of Manila. In this respect, the *Noli* is the literary equivalent of the articles of the propagandists from *La Solidaridad*. Second, the novel represents Rizal's desire to abandon the egoist politics of agitators past. In Ibarra, we have the figure of the reformer who has not sufficiently tied his liberal politics to self-abnegation and sacrifice. Third, and most importantly, we see in the novel Rizal's contention that selfless patriotism and pain purifies the naïve liberal's intent.

BIBLIOGRAPHY

Abinales, Patricio N., and Donna J. Amoroso. 2017. *State and Society in the Philippines*. 2nd ed. Quezon City: Ateneo de Manila University Press.

Anderson, Benedict R.O'G. 1998. *The Spectre of Comparisons: Nationalism, Southeast Asia, and the World*. New York: Verso.

Castroverde, Aaron C. 2013. *Jose Rizal and the Spanish Novel*. PhD Dissertation, Duke University.

Daroy, Petronilo Bn. 1968. Crisostomo Ibarra. In *Rizal: Contrary Essays*, ed. Petronilo Bn. Daroy and Dolores S. Feria. Quezon City: Guro Books.

Guerrero, Leon Ma. 2012. *The First Filipino: A Biography of Jose Rizal*. Makati City: Guerrero Publishing.

Hau, Caroline S. 2000. *Necessary Fictions: Philippine Literature and the Nation, 1946–1980*. Quezon City: Ateneo de Manila University Press.

———. 2004. *On the Subject of the Nation: Filipino Writings from the Margins, 1981–2004*. Quezon City: Ateneo de Manila University Press.

————. 2017. Did Padre Damaso Rape Pia Alba?: Reticence, Revelation, and Revolution in Jose Rizal's Novels. *Philippine Studies: Historical and Ethnographic Viewpoints* 65 (2): 137–199.

Joaquin, Nick. 2005. *A Question of Heroes.* Pasig City: Anvil Publishing Inc.

Mojares, Resil B. 1983. *Origins and Rise of the Filipino Novel: A Generic Study of the Novel Until 1940.* Quezon City: University of the Philippines Press.

————. 2013. *Isabelo's Archive.* Manila: Anvil Publishing Inc.

Ocampo, Ambeth R. 2012. *Rizal Without the Overcoat.* Pasig City: Anvil Publishing Inc.

Palma, Rafael. 1949. *Biografia de Rizal.* Manila: Bureau of Print.

Quibuyen, Floro. 1997. Rizal and the Revolution. *Philippine Studies: Historical and Ethnographic Viewpoints* 45 (2): 225–257.

Retana, Wenceslao. 1907. *Vida y Escritos Del Dr. Jose Rizal.* Madrid: Liberaria General de V. Suarez.

Schumacher, John N. 1997. *The Propaganda Movement: 1880–1895: The Creation of a Filipino Consciousness, the Making of a Revolution.* Quezon City: Ateneo de Manila University Press.

CHAPTER 4

The Solution of the Enigma in
El Filibusterismo

Abstract This chapter examines Rizal's second, more incendiary novel, *El Filibusterismo*. If the *Noli* was an experiment in liberal reformism, the *Fili* is an experiment in revolution. Using the character of Simoun—the radicalized Ibarra who goes home to the Philippines to foment an insurrection—Rizal tests the viability of revolution in the Philippines. Like Ibarra's school, Simoun's revolution is a failure. This chapter concludes that the *Fili* is an intentionally ambiguous novel—a novel that refuses to make recommendations about revolutionary violence, but rather poses Socratic questions about how a people should earn their liberty.

Keywords *El Filibusterismo* • Rizal • Liberalism • Revolution • Subversion

Noli Me Tangere ends with questions, the biggest one centered on its main character, Ibarra, who vows to return as a *verdadero filibustero*, a true subversive. The foreshadowing in the *Noli* and the title of the second novel signal Rizal's intentions for continuing his story: he wishes to explore the themes of subversion, criminality, and revolution.

Rizal had been thinking about the meaning of filibustero years before he wrote his second novel. And he knew that the term's meaning changed depending on context. Despite its evolving meaning, however, it was a

© The Author(s) 2019
L. E. Claudio, *Jose Rizal*, Global Political Thinkers,
https://doi.org/10.1007/978-3-030-01316-5_4

consistent way for colonial authority to mark individuals as undesirable and turn them into political outcasts. In the year of the *Noli*'s publication, Rizal wrote Blumentritt to explain the term:

> The word filibustero is little known in the Philippines. The masses do not know it yet. I heard it for the first time in 1872 when the tragic executions took place. I still remember the panic that this word created. Our father forbade us to utter it, as well as the words Cavite, Burgos, (one of the executed priests), *etc.* The Manila newspapers and the Spaniards apply this word to one whom they want to make a revolutionary suspect. The Filipinos belonging to the educated class fear the reach of the word. It does not have the meaning of freebooters; it rather means a dangerous man who will soon be *hanged* or well, a *presumptuous man* (emphasis in original). (Letters to Blumentritt, 69)

Over three years later, it was Blumentritt's (1891, 59) turn to forward a theory of *filibusterismo* in the pages of *La Solidaridad*, arguing:

> Since the independence of the colonies in America, all Spaniards—friars, army men and civilians continued to impute filibusterism to every movement or tendency of the Filipinos. This mania to seek filibusterism where there is none has now reached a stage where every intelligent and educated Filipino is regarded as a filibustero with the result that the educated Filipinos do not talk about their country's problems for fear they would endanger not only their lives but also those of all their relatives.

The label *filibustero* was therefore slippery, and therein lay its danger.[1] Any enemy—and in 1872 it was the nationalist priests—could become a filibustero. For Rizal, however, the priests were not true *filibusteros*. In the first pages of the *Fili,* he turns to Fathers Gomez, Burgos, and Zamora, and dedicates the novel to their memory. "So since no one has truly shown in any manner your participation in the Cavite uprising," he wrote, "I feel I have the right to dedicate my work to the victims of the evil I'm struggling against" (Fili, xxiv). Falsely accused, the priests were not *verdaderos filibusteros*. Falsely accused as well, neither Ibarra was a *verdadero filibustero*. So what constitutes true subversion? And what would a true subversive espouse?

---

[1] For a history of the shifting meanings of the word, from its associations with piracy to its political use during Rizal's time, see Filomeno Aguilar (2011).

The answer might lie in a mysterious quote from Blumentritt's *La Solidaridad* essay that Rizal reproduced in the dedication page of the *Fili*:

> One could easily imagine that some subversive person has secretly bewitched the alliance of friars and reactionaries to make them continue to follow impulses that unwittingly foster and foment a politics that pursues a single objective: the extension of subversive ideas throughout the country. They will end up convincing every last Filipino that the only salvation is separation from the Mother Country. (*Fili*, xxv)

The quote represents Blumentritt's flight of fancy. And this fantastic idea inspired Rizal to write his darkest character.

SENTIMENT VERSUS THOUGHT

The *Fili* does not receive as much attention as the *Noli*, perhaps because of its heavy-handedness and its comparative lack of humor and satire. Retana (1907, 201) notes that the first novel is a work of "emotion" (*sentida*), "a picture of the entire country, rich in color and fantasy, blended with the dreams of a sensitive poet." Meanwhile, the sequel is a work of "thought" (*pensada*), "a series of philosophical/political treaties in the form of fiction," where "every speech" becomes "a nationalist dissertation."[2] Rizal could, indeed, be prone to letting his political purpose override stylistic concerns, himself conceding: "As for me, the question of writing in more or less literary style is secondary; the principal thing is to think and feel rightly, work with purpose, and the pen will take care of transmitting it" (Reformists, 173). For critics like Retana, the *Fili*'s weakness lies in its prioritization of political purpose over literary style.

Another possible reason for the *Fili*'s comparative lack of prominence is its difficulty as a text. Rizal asks questions in the *Noli*, but does not provide direct answers in the *Fili*. The *Noli* excoriates Ibarra's politics, and we expect Rizal to outline a concrete political project in his next novel. But, as we shall see, he does not.

Despite its inadequacies, Rizal was proud of his second novel, viewing it as an improvement over the first. As it was about to go to press, Rizal claimed that he wrote it "with more ardor than the Noli and though it is not so cheerful, at least it is more profound and more perfect" (Reformists 563).

---

[2] Translation from Spanish mine.

The *Fili* represents the advances in Rizal's political thought in the latter half of his career, a time when he had settled on two related beliefs: first, the pro-independence position that liberal reform was impossible under Spanish colonialism and, second, the idea that the propaganda movement needed to be brought back to the Philippines.

Like the *Noli* before it, the *Fili* represents the Philippines faithfully, with the goal of letting the reader make empirically valid assessments of the colony's politics. Its events occur 13 years after the first novel (placing it in 1896 or earlier), and center around the figure of a mysterious jeweler, Simoun, a gray eminence behind a draconian Governor General of the Philippines. Simoun, we immediately discover, is Ibarra, who has returned to the Philippines after traveling primarily across South America.

There is a sense that the stakes are higher in the *Fili*. For all its complexity, the *Noli* focuses on the town of San Diego, and the narrator himself accepts his own restricted, provincial purview by claiming, "we know few people in Manila" (*Noli*, 382). In the *Fili*, however, we spend more time in the capital, and, through Simoun, we eavesdrop on the conversations between high government officials and friars more so than we did in the *Noli*. There is also a shift in the narrator's tone, now more somber and less sarcastic.

Since the authorities believe Ibarra dead, nobody knows Simon's true identity, except for the medical student Basilio—a character from the previous novel. In the *Noli*, Basilio's mother, Sisa, is driven to madness after the disappearance of her younger son, Crispin (likely murdered in Father Salvi's Church).[3] The strain of loss is too much for Sisa, and Basilio finds her dying in the large forest of the Ibarra family. There, Basilio also finds the dying Elias. Ibarra appears and helps Basilio bury the two corpses. In the *Fili*, Basilio is the ward of Captain Tiago. In one of the early chapters, Basilio visits his mother's grave only to find the jeweler in the same spot, and we discover that Simoun and Crisostomo Ibarra are one and the same.

There are two projects, two new experiments at the center of the *Fili*'s plot. On the one hand, a group of reformist Manila students, including Basilio, espouse educational reform by lobbying the government to build a Castilian language academy for students in Manila. The other experiment is that of Simoun, who influences the Governor General and other government officials to restrict civil liberties and inflict various acts of repression. In furthering the corruption of the government, Simoun hopes to

[3] The novel is vague as to who killed Crispin.

foment anger that would trigger insurrections. Through abetting and encouraging corruption and oppression, Simoun hopes to hasten the overthrow of the government, and to exact revenge on his enemies. While pushing the government toward draconian governance, Simoun is simultaneously organizing a revolution. And in this plot he has a number of co-conspirators: There is peasant leader Cabesang Tales, a resident of San Diego pushed out of his land by avaricious friars. There is the Chinese businessman Quiroga, in whose house Simoun stores his arms. Eventually, Simoun recruits Basilio, after the latter is jailed for joining meetings of the reformist students.

In the beginning, the *Fili* seems set in the Philippines of the authoritarian, reactionary Governor General Valeriano Weyler. Anderson (2007, 108) notes that the "oafish, brutal and cynical Su Exelencia" is based on Weyler, "the future butcher of Cuba," while the liberal Captain General who opposes him is modeled on a Manila civil governor. The injustices committed by friars to Cabesang Tales, who eventually becomes the bandit Matanglawin, are similar to those committed against Rizal's family and others in the town of Calamba (the friars increase rents steadily until Tales is threatened with eviction and must defend his land) (ibid., 109). Finally, the student reformists are similar in their fecklessness to Rizal's old *La Solidaridad* comrades, with the key difference that they are not overseas (ibid.).

But the introduction of Simoun makes us doubt that these events occur in the exact present. Unlike Ibarra whose reformism was based on the creole liberals of previous decades, there was no antecedent for a nihilistic, anarchic character who wished to push the corruption of the colonial government to the point of implosion. Even his name alludes to the sense of disjointedness he creates. In romantic poetry, the "simoun wind was an exemplary figure of the sublime because, as a force of nature capable of visiting violence and destruction on humans and obliterating individual and cultural (including national) subjectivity, the simoun resisted the European (imperialist) attempt to inscribe if not impose European cultural values on the desert landscape" (Hau 2017, 175). Simoun is from outside the geography of national community, and maybe even outside its temporality.

The biggest difference between the *Noli* and the *Fili* is that the former represents a history of creole liberal reformists past, while the latter tests a possible revolution in the near horizon. The ending of the *Noli* is foretold in the histories of figures such as Burgos, while the *Fili*'s is not. It is Rizal's own vision of what could be. The *Noli* was published in 1887 and, as established in the previous chapter, it was set roughly in 1883 or earlier, making it an account of the past. The *Fili*, on the other hand, was published in 1891 and, if we assume that the Noli occurred in 1883, its events transpire in 1896, the year of the Philippine Revolution (the novel explicitly states that it happens 13 years after). At the very least, the *Fili* is set in Rizal's present; at most, it is set in the near future.

THE FAILURE OF LIBERAL *MEDIATION*

Like the *Noli*, the second novel is filled with various characters, some real and others more archetypal. For our purposes, however, let us begin with a minor character, who is nevertheless crucial to the plot. Toward the end of the first half of the novel, the students decide that the success of their Spanish academy hinges on recruiting an effective mediator to convince the friars and high government officials. Since their petition concerned language instruction, its fate would be in the hands of the Select Committee on Primary Instruction. Fortunately, the students thought, the committee would be headed by the liberal Don Custodio, whom they believed would be their ally. "If we are able to influence Don Custodio's will, so that in following his liberal bent, he recommends on our behalf," claims the leader Macaraig, "we'll win it all" (*Fili*, 122).

Six chapters later, the narrator profiles Custodio in a chapter titled "The Arbitrator." The English translation is adequate, but fails to capture the complexity of the original Spanish *Ponente*, which refers not just to a mediator, but also someone who takes account of a situation and proposes solutions. A *ponente* may also be a rapporteur or someone who speaks in favor of a case. We may also glean meaning from Custodio's name—custodian. For the students, Custodio is a custodian not just of the future of their academy, but also of the liberalism they seek to bring to the Philippines.[4]

Custodio fails as both a *ponente* and a custodian of liberalism. Succumbing to reactionary friars, not only does he refuse to lobby for the students, he also abets their arrests. The friars and government brand the students "filibusteros" with nary a word from the "liberal" Custodio. For their efforts, the main conspirators end up in jail. And while the wealthy

[4] I am indebted to Caroline Hau for these insights on the term *ponente* and the relevance of Custodio's name.

ones in the group have friends in high places who negotiate their release, it is the lower class Basilio who spends the most time incarcerated.

As we saw in Chap. 2, Spanish liberals succumbing to friar power is a consistent theme in Rizal. In becoming pawns of the reaction, they become hypocrites, liberals only in name. That Rizal saw Don Custodio this way is evidenced by his sarcastic description of the mediator's liberalism, noting that:

> Since he was so proud of his liberalism, when he was asked what he thought of indios, he would respond as if he were doing someone a great favor, that they were fine for mechanical work and the imitative arts—by which he meant music, painting and sculpture—adding his usual coda that to truly understand them you had to spend a great many years in the country. (*Fili*, 173)

As an act of pride, Custodio displays "liberalism," and uses it to patronize the locals, stripping liberalism of its political content and turning it into a fashionable label and signal of sophistication— "liberalism" as flaneurial politics. Yet Custodio backs off from the more controversial elements of his political creed. While in Spain, he "had spoken badly of the religious orders to avoid discord in the circles in which he moved." But in the Philippines, he would "extend the hand of friendship to the highness of mystery" and declare that friars are "a necessary evil." In colonial contexts, the narrator quips, "A liberal can—and must—be a Catholic where reactionaries miss gods and saints, the way a mulatto can pass for white in Kaffir" (*Fili*, 173). The line's racism notwithstanding, the implication is that Custodio only passes for a "liberal" in the context of reactionary Philippines.

Once again we are faced with Rizal's portrait of liberals who cannot uphold their beliefs in the colony, like those he pilloried in his letters and like the main character of his first novel. We do not know if Custodio is based on a specific individual, but it is likely that Rizal used him to represent the hypocritical Spanish liberal that he decries in his essays—those who "asphyxiate" their beliefs in Manila. As in these texts, Rizal's qualm in *Fili* is not with liberalism *per se*, but with liberal Spaniards who are not brave enough to stick to their principles.

Through the story of the idealistic students, Rizal rehearses a theme from the *Noli*: the impossibility of liberal reformism in a country dominated by friars. Through the character of Custodio, he nuances this insight: Not only will the friars block liberalism, so-called Spanish liberals will abet them. The uselessness of the Spanish liberal custodian means that Filipinos had to take matters into their own hands.

There is, therefore, some wisdom in the filibustero Simoun—a wisdom that stems from his disillusionment with liberal reform amid Spanish colonialism. Rizal uses Simoun's voice to mock his colleagues in Spain who continued to ask for Hispanization. In an oft-quoted line, he tells Basilio, "Go ahead, ask for your equal rights and the Hispanization of your customs and see what you'll get: the death of your nationality, the annihilation of your homeland, and the consecration of tyranny." The future for reformist Filipinos, he argued, was "a nation without liberty" (*Fili*, 53).

The story of the Spanish academy is a reminder of Ibarra's arch. And with Basilio experiencing a disillusionment similar to that of Ibarra/Simoun, he now becomes willing to join Simoun in his insurrection. But this insurrection is likewise a failure.

NITROGLYCERIN

Simoun's schemes climax with a plan to bomb a wedding in what was once Captain Tiago's (now deceased) house. He plants explosives in the house, and gifts the couple a lamp charged with nitroglycerin that will detonate once ignited. Knowing the plan, Basilio warns his friend Isagani to stay away from the party. But Isagani, who is in love with the bride, throws the lamp into the river before it explodes. Eventually, Father Salvi intuits that Simoun is Ibarra and the mastermind of the attempted bombing. After being pursued by the Civil Guard, a wounded Simoun flees.

In the novel's closing chapters, Simoun, who has poisoned himself, is dying in the home of a Filipino priest, Fr. Florentino. Through Florentino, Rizal explains why Simoun's revolution failed, with the priest saying:

> The glory of saving a country doesn't mean having to use the measures that contributed to its ruin! You have believed that what crime and iniquity have stained and deformed, another crime and another iniquity can purify and redeem! That's wrong! Hatred creates nothing but monsters. Only love can bring about wondrous things. Only virtue is redemptive. No, if someday our country can be free, it will not be by vice and crime, not by corruption of our children, by cheating some, and buying others. No, redemption supposes virtue, sacrifice, and sacrifice, love! (*Fili*, 324)

What then is to be done? Consistent with the theme of pain, suffering, and liberty in Rizal's thinking, the Filipino priest declares that "The just and the worthy have to suffer in order to spread their ideas and let them be known." Those who seek justice for their country, he concludes, must "Suffer and work" (*Fili*, 324). After Simoun dies, Fr. Florentino casts his jewels into the sea, and the novel appears to draw a definitive anti-revolutionary conclusion.

Yet Benedict Anderson (2007, 120) argues that readers should not take Florentino's words as Rizal's final position. First, he notes that Simoun does not respond to the priest's mini homily, and that he neither confesses his sins nor asks forgiveness. Second, he points out that, in the third to the last chapter, Isagani, when asked about the person who foiled Simoun's plans (Isagani himself), flashes an "enigmatic" smile and declares: "If that thief had known what it was all about and had been able to think about it, he definitely would have done it" (*Fili*, 312). It is as if, Anderson (2007, 121) concludes, Rizal is considering another sequel.

Anderson's reading, which tries to establish the radical, anarchist influences on Rizal's thinking, distances the *Fili* from reformism, paying more attention to the winks and the feints in the text, instead of the large picture: Simoun's revolution fails and the final word in a chapter titled "Conclusion" is that of a Filipino priest, categorically condemning the filibustero's actions. Isagani's statement, to be sure, is a playful what-if, but it by no means clarifies Rizal's thoughts on violence and revolution. Anderson is nevertheless correct that the *Fili* is "proleptic" (ibid.) in that the text carries a sense of trembling expectation of something to yet come (ibid., 122). What the *Fili* anticipates, however, is ephemeral and indeterminate. The novel is certainly proleptic, but, more importantly, it is enigmatic.

"THE SOLUTION OF THE ENIGMA"

The *Noli* ended with a question—one that readers may have expected a more categorical answer to in the sequel. But even if the *Fili* brings to a close the story of Juan Crisostomo Ibarra/Simoun, it still refuses to offer a cure to the social cancer described in the first novel—an inconclusiveness that may be both the novel's greatest defect and merit. One of the earliest criticisms of the novel came from Rizal's *La Solidaridad* colleague Graciano Lopez Jaena, who admired the book and found it superior to the *Noli*. Despite his admiration of its artistic virtues, however, Jaena found the novel's ending deficient. Writing to Rizal in 1891, he said that "in your magnificent work you have closed the doors, the exit, with your resort to confusing argumentation, sowing, at the conclusion, anxiety in the hearts, darkness, doubt, and incredulity in the minds, easy of being dissipated, clarified and comprehended by brains accustomed to think, but impossible of being understood by minds which have just opened to the light, like those of our people." Few, he contended, would guess at the "solution of the enigma" Rizal presented (Reformists 611).

Jaena voiced his criticism privately and told Rizal that, in public, he would "stress the beauties of the book." He also understood that Rizal "wished to leave to the Filipino people the solution of their social and political problems" (ibid., 611). Such an approach would have, indeed, been consistent with the *Noli*'s goal of letting the Filipinos collectively propose cures to the illness of their nation. Still, Jaena was right about the novel being confusing. It remains the case today.

The indeterminacy stems from Rizal's own ambivalent position, which oscillated between the militancy of Simoun and the caution of Florentino. Rizal was never categorical about his thoughts on revolutionary violence. Joaquin (2005, 55) explains that "The Hamlet split in Rizal between the will to act and the tendency to scruple preceded the flagrant schizophrenia of *El Filibusterismo*." Rizal's thoughts about revolution were always fickle. Or as he said in the early 1880s, "My life has been one of continuous doubting and continues vacillation" (PHW, 10).

At his angriest, Rizal could write in a voice like Simoun's, as when he wrote to Mariano Ponce in 1889, recalling his anger after the events of 1872. Writing to Ponce, he anticipates Simoun with a wish that the authorities turn more draconian:

> May they commit abuses, let there be imprisonments, banishments, executions, good. Let Destiny be fulfilled! The day they lay their hands on us, the day they martyrize innocent families for our fault, goodbye, friar government, and perhaps, goodbye Spanish government! (Reformists, 321)

Rizal understood the possibility of revolt because he had studied the history of liberalism, adding that "The cruelties and selfishness of Louis XIV and XV brought about the Revolution; the cruelties of the Inquisition killed monasticism" (ibid.). In an undated essay, likely from 1894, he even entertained the possibility of a violent liberal revolution. How might liberals win against the friars he asked? "If tired persecuted, and desperate," he argued, they may "throw all caution to the wind" and, arming themselves like their Spanish counterparts, "behead their enemies" as vengeance "for acts that they call violent and brutal, for so many imprisonments, exiles, and executions committed" (PHW, 14).

But at his most circumspect, he spoke like Florentino, and there is no better example of this than his trial defense statement from 1896 where he wrote: "I knew that through arms it was impossible to win liberties and less independence" (PHW, 345). As with Florentino, he preached the need for cultivating virtues over revolutionary violence:

> I would like the Filipino people to become worthy, noble, honorable, for a people who makes itself despicable for its cowardice or vices exposes itself to abuses and vexations. Man in general oppresses what he despises, and this is what I used to say to those who complained to me: "If we were more worthy, they would not do that to us." (ibid.)

That Rizal could echo the positions of multiple characters not only speak to the fact that novelists sprinkle different parts of their personalities unto different characters. In the case of Rizal's position vis-à-vis Simoun and Florentino, one must think of his oscillating position as an attempt at a dialectic. On the one hand, pain brings about liberty, and the liberal must assume that suffering is part of progress. On the other, it is sheer Machiavellianism to abet social suffering as a way of exposing the existing fissures of a society. And more importantly, the right to liberal revolt is earned by not only one's experience of pain but also one's vision of what replaces this pain.

Despite his flirtation with Jacobin insurrection, when we take Rizal's writings and career as a whole, we see that he gave more of his voice to Fr. Florentino than to Simoun. At the very least, we know that he deeply admired the man on whom he modeled Florentino—a certain Fr. Leoncio Lopez, a Filipino priest, who was his father's best friend. Writing to Blumentritt, Rizal claimed that Lopez "was a just, liberal, and tolerant man. You will see his portrait in my new book; I call him Father Florentino" (Letters to Blumentritt, 414).

Simoun, on the other hand, was a dark and morally compromised character. In a letter to Marcelo H. del Pilar, his rival as leader of the Filipino expatriates, he revealed the logic of writing the Simoun character. While writing the *Fili*, Rizal was embroiled in a public spat between del Pilar and other members of *La Solidaridad* over issues of leadership and strategy. Trying to dispel accusations that he was vindictive toward del Pilar and *La Solidaridad*, Rizal claimed that it "was my purpose in making Simoun a dark figure in order to show that those of *La Solidaridad* are not *filibuste-ros*" (Reformists, 681). Simoun is then a heuristic, a way for us to rethink the ways in which Philippine society viewed *filibusterismo*.

Simoun is the *verdadero filibustero*, and the others—the students in the novel wishing to build a Spanish academy and the real-life propagandists of *La Solidaridad* who lobbied for reforms in Europe—were merely labeled *filibusteros* by the friars. Though he likely saw these students as naïve—possibly because, as Anderson (2007, 110) notes, these students were "a microcosmic version of the tactical assimilation campaign conducted by Del Pilar" and the remaining expatriate movement—he insisted that Simoun is the social threat.

Not only is Simoun darker than any previous character. There is also no foil to his politics, except for the feeble Basilio, who becomes a co-conspirator in the end. Unlike the *Noli*, there are no models of self-sacrificing patriots like Elias in the *Fili*. Fr. Florentino is thinking about patriots who will work and suffer for the country, but they are nowhere to be found in the novel's pages. And although Florentino echoes many of Elias's views about self-sacrifice, the priest does not perform an act of heroic sacrifice himself. *El Filibusterismo*, as the title implies, is about Simoun, about *filibusterismo*. Jaena was correct to note that the solutions in the novel were enigmatic, even more enigmatic than in the *Noli*, which at least held up Elias as a model of patriotism.

A JUST REVOLUTION?

But are there political models that we can glean when we read between the lines of a politically ambivalent novel? If the *Noli*'s goal was to expose the social cancer, to diagnose it even further without even hinting at cures, it then becomes redundant. And some parts are, for sure, redundant, especially since Florentino's homily on sacrifice reads like rehash of ideas from the fallen Elias. Having killed that character, it is as if Rizal tried to reintroduce him once more. But the difference between the *Noli* and the *Fili* is that the latter directly tackles the issue of revolution. As we noted earlier, both novels have parallel structures, with the *Noli* being Ibarra's experiment in liberal reformism and the *Fili* being Simoun's experiment in revolution.

A question that has bedeviled much of the scholarship on Rizal is a facile one: Did he or did he not endorse revolution? Was he a counter-revolutionary? In 1969, Renato Constantino (2005), one of the purveyors of the new nationalist historiography of the era, condemned Rizal and his liberalism on the basis of his rejection of the Katipunan, claiming:

> Since his idea of liberty was essentially the demand for those rights which the elite needed in order to prosper economically, Rizal did not consider political independence as a prerequisite to freedom. Fearful of the violence of people's action, he did not want us to fight for our independence.

Floro Quibuyen (1997) refutes Constantino's claims that Rizal rejected the Katipunan, but nevertheless accepts the premise that Rizal's legacy is best judged on his position on the Katipunan's revolution, chiding Constantino for uncritically accepting the popular belief that Rizal was "a counter-revolutionary bourgeois intellectual" (ibid., 254). Unfortunately, this debate rests on how well historians are able to place Rizal within pseudo-Marxist boxes of bourgeois and proletarian, revolutionary and counter-revolutionary. But this was not the way liberals of Rizal's generation assessed revolutionary violence.

The simplistic question of did he or did he not support revolution is absurd because few reformists are absolute pacifists, who reject the violent overthrow of governments at all costs. Likewise, few revolutionaries are so trigger happy as to launch violent campaigns at every opportunity. If the *Fili* is complex and ambiguous, it is because it serves as a Socratic decision-making guide for its reader. For surely Rizal knew that his audience consisted of Filipinos who, like him, had decided that independence was the only long-term solution to the country's ills. And Rizal also understood that terror could accompany revolutions—that these movements could devour their own children.

In 1889, as he was writing the *Fili*, Rizal told Ponce the God and Destiny were on the side of the propagandists "because we are fighting not for selfish reasons but for the sacred love of our country and compatriots." Many of those who preceded them "fought for their own interests and so God did not support them." What made Rizal's cause just was the fight for "more justice and more liberty and for the sacred rights of man" (Reformists, 353). This cause was not based on hate or bloodlust, as a "resort to force" would only become necessary "when we have exhausted all means, when they drive us to the wall." At which point Filipinos, "like the North Americans," would "fight for our just cause, and we shall triumph" (ibid.). We are certain, therefore, that Rizal was capable of endorsing and even celebrating a violent liberal revolution, like that of the creoles of North America.

From this letter, we can extrapolate the two conditions under which Rizal would have endorsed revolutionary violence. First, that it be the last resort, with all means exhausted. Second, that revolution not be motivated by individual self-interest but by values of universal justice and rights. In other words, adherence to liberal principles determined the viability of a revolutionary movement. It is in this context that we must interpret Fr. Florentino's claim that "as long as our country is not ready, as long as they enter the fight under false pretenses or are pushed into it, without a clear consciousness of what must be done, even the wisest attempts will fail and better that they fail because why give a groom a wife whom he doesn't love adequately, for whom he is not ready to die?" (*Fili*, 326).

Why did Simoun's experiment in revolutionary insurrection fail? Was it because it was violent? Was it because it failed to consider the value of reform? Unlikely, because the author of *Noli me Tangere* was aware of reformism's limits. More probably, it was because one's quest for selfish revenge does not constitute a liberal struggle. If a nation were to emerge from the work of propagandists and/or revolutionaries, it would be because they shared common principles.

What then constitutes a national community? At his worst, Rizal could be racialist about his conceptions of a nation, seeing the Philippines through a Malayan lens, glorifying the precolonial achievements of his "race" (Aguilar 2005; Ocampo 2013, 75–117).[5] But race-oriented propaganda notwithstanding, Rizal was aware that common political ideals determined the coherence of a nation. As he was beginning work on *El Filibusterismo*, he wrote that "Neither obscurantism and fanaticism, nor oppression or superstitions ever bind nor have they ever bound peoples. On the other hand, liberty, rights, and love group distinct races around the same standard, one aspiration, one destiny" (PHW, 81). Like the American founding fathers, Rizal's nationalist vision was founded on creed and not ethnicity.

The goal of Rizal was neither reformism nor revolution, but the formation of a liberal republic. We will never know for certain what his preferred method for achieving this liberal republic was. As Hau (2017, 177)

---

[5] In his defense, however, his racialist rhetoric was largely a reaction to Spanish racism which denigrated the indio. As Guerrero (2012, 238) notes, Rizal's "ear was cocked vigilantly for any criticism of the Philippines or the Filipinos, any sneer, any innuendo, and as soon as he heard it he was on his feet, crying to be recognized, to reply, to point out errors and contradictions, to unmask motives, to expose malice and corruption."

explains, "the *Fili* leaves open the questions of what kind and extent of reform—with revolution as the 'ultimate reason' (la última razón), the final means by which people insist on bringing about change—are needed to break the cycle of oppression and retribution and how to offer some measure of institutional safeguards against incalculable violence." The quest to find definitive meaning in Rizal's novels is understandable, especially for Filipino nationalists who treat his work as holy writ. But foreclosing interpretative possibilities blunts the power of Rizal's work. We may attempt to pigeonhole the liberal, but the complexity of his texts will leave us in doubt. Jaena was confounded, and so must we.

CONCLUSION

The *Fili* is the more challenging of Rizal's novels because it seeks to do more than document the failure and impossibility of liberal reform under colonialism. As a meditation on subversion, it asks multiple questions about the future of the Philippines that the author cannot directly answer. What is the revolutionary breaking point for Filipinos? Can revolutionary movements move a community closer to this point by enhancing the "vexations" of colonial rule? When is bloodshed justified?

Rizal's novels, the *Fili* in particular, leave us with difficult questions. They remain unanswered either because the author decided to withdraw those answers, or because he did not have them himself. This uncertainty only reflects the uncertainty inherent in Rizal's avowed philosophy of liberalism: The liberal asks tough questions and thinks these questions through without the certainty of definitive conclusions. If the liberal is accused of being fickle, it is because he is—his mind perennially balancing competing truth claims that require a modus vivendi. He is also haunted by the question of terror, since he does not easily scoff at the great loss of life. Such was the burden of deliberation that Rizal carried on his shoulders.

BIBLIOGRAPHY

Aguilar, Filomeno V. 2005. Tracing Origins: Ilustrado Nationalism and the Racial Science of Migration Waves. *The Journal of Asian Studies* 64 (03): 605–637.
———. 2011. Filibustero, Rizal, and the Manilamen of the Nineteenth Century. *Philippine Studies* 59 (4): 429–469.
Anderson, Benedict R.O'G. 2007. *Under Three Flags: Anarchism and the Anti-Colonial Imagination*. Pasig City: Anvil Publishing Inc.

Blumentritt, Ferdinand. 1891. Sketches. *La Solidaridad* Year 3, no. 49. In *La Solidaridad*, vol. 3, Trans. Guadalupe Fores-Ganzon. Pasig City: Fundacion Santiago, 1996.

Constantino, Renato. 2005. Veneration Without Understanding. *The Philippine Reporter*, June 16. http://philippinereporter.com/2005/06/16/veneration-without-understanding/

Guerrero, Leon Ma. 2012. *The First Filipino: A Biography of Jose Rizal*. Makati City: Guerrero Publishing.

Hau, Caroline S. 2017. Did Padre Damaso Rape Pia Alba?: Reticence, Revelation, and Revolution in Jose Rizal's Novels. *Philippine Studies: Historical and Ethnographic Viewpoints* 65 (2): 137–199.

Joaquin, Nick. 2005. *A Question of Heroes*. Pasig City: Anvil Publishing Inc.

Ocampo, Ambeth R. 2013. *Meaning and History: The Rizal Lectures*. Revised ed. Pasig City: Anvil Publishing Inc.

Quibuyen, Floro. 1997. Rizal and the Revolution. *Philippine Studies: Historical and Ethnographic Viewpoints* 45 (2): 225–257.

Retana, Wenceslao. 1907. *Vida y Escritos Del Dr. Jose Rizal*. Madrid: Liberaria General de V. Suarez.

CHAPTER 5

Conclusion: Resurrecting Plants

Abstract This conclusion asks what Rizal's vision of liberalism means for postcolonies and the Global South today. It critiques the tendency among postcolonial scholars to treat liberalism as the "Other" of their radical project from the margins. Their writings fail to acknowledge the contributions of postcolonial liberals like Rizal in forming independent political communities. Finally, it contends that a renewed liberalism is necessary amid the rise of global populism and illiberal democracy.

Keywords Postcolonial theory • Liberalism • Global South • Populism • Illiberal democracy • Duterte

Too often, with liberalism, we throw the baby out with the bathwater. In contemporary critical and cultural theory, criticisms of liberalism are almost mandatory. This is most true in the field of postcolonial theory or in philosophies of the Global South. For many postcolonial scholars, "western" liberalism is the common enemy of the politics and ideas from the margins of global knowledge production. At times, one may be led to think that, without liberalism as a common target, postcolonial theory would lose its cohesion. Postcolonies are, after all, different, and the philosophies their intellectuals have espoused have likewise been varied.

© The Author(s) 2019
L. E. Claudio, *Jose Rizal*, Global Political Thinkers,
https://doi.org/10.1007/978-3-030-01316-5_5

Without a positive notion of theory from the Global South, scholars have turned to denigrating "liberal" modernity.[1]

Of course, some anti-liberal scholarship has surfaced dark legacies of the European tradition. But even these turn critique into blanket dismissal. For example, the scathing work of Uday Singh Mehta (1999) proves how British liberal intellectuals like Jeremy Benthan, James and John Stuart Mill, and Lord Macaulay defended imperialism, particularly in India. The idea of Western tutelage for "backward" societies, he contends, stems from the liberal embrace of universal values to the exclusion of different cultures and belief systems. Hence, "the liberal involvement with the British Empire is broadly coeval with liberalism itself" (ibid., 4). Echoing Mehta, the sociologist Julian Go (2017, 74) contends that "civic-liberal nations" are *"empire-states"* (emphasis in original) because they "are predicated upon a core hierarchized binary of citizen and Other— that is, between those who are members of the community because they are rational, mature, and civilized, and those who are not."

These scholars are sympathetic to the concerns of postcolonies and the Global South. But they have unwittingly wedded themselves to the study of the Global North. In studying liberalism, they privilege the voices of liberals from Europe, while neglecting how liberalism has been articulated in postcolonies themselves. A global history of liberalism must acknowledge the contributions of colonial thinkers in its development. True enough, we may condemn thinkers like Mill for their defense of imperialism, but we must also celebrate their counterpoints from within the liberal tradition. We must celebrate thinkers like Rizal.

Rizal would have accepted many of the objections of scholars like Mehta and Go. He too knew how liberals from colonial metropoles could use their ideas to support colonialism. But Rizal would have rejected the reduction of liberalism's vast history to the actions of colonizers. In this book, I hope to have shown that, while Rizal criticized Spanish liberals, he never abandoned the liberal project. Rather, he believed that liberalism could be renewed, even purified, in the colony, through the painful experiences of colonials like himself.

Rizal too would not have dismissed liberalism simply because it could create "Others." For he knew that any political community needs to have an inside and an outside: nations have foreigners, religions have non-believers, and socialist movements have class enemies. In this regard,

[1] See Claudio 2017 for a critical summary of the illiberalism of works on the Global South.

liberalism is no different from other political ideals that form bonds of community. Rizal knew, however, that the bonds of community within liberal republics could be expansive and cosmopolitan. He saw how the category "Filipino" could expand from only referring to creoles to include all those who identified with the emergent nation. He believed in communities not bound by race or religion, but adherence to Enlightenment philosophy.

Such a worldview is simple, but it comes to us with a certain urgency today, at a time when "illiberal democracy" is one the rise. For much of the post-Cold War world, progressive and radical thinkers insisted that there was more to human political development than the mere liberal "end of history." There had to be more radical ways to imagining politics. Amid this desire, much anti-liberal thinking became nihilistic, and those who condemned liberalism rarely thought of concrete alternatives. At worse, they denigrated the basic tenets of liberalism, without care for the possible repercussions.

The disillusionment with liberalism is, of course, nothing new. Even as Rizal was articulating a liberalism for the colonized in the nineteenth century, many Europeans were already becoming sick of the liberal project. Francois Furet (2000, 11) explains that many radicals from that period had come to believe "that modern liberal democracy was threatening society with dissolution because it atomized individuals, made them indifferent to public interest, weakened authority, and encouraged class hatred." This disillusionment would eventually lead to the twin illiberal philosophies that dominated the twentieth century: fascism on the right and Communism on the Left.

History, of course, does not repeat itself. But there are echoes of the illiberal early twentieth century today. If the present moment prompts comparisons with the 1930s and 1940s, it is not because we are about to enter another period of global warfare. Rather, it is because, our present, like those years, teems with illiberalism. And, like the early twentieth century, intellectuals in the West have been averse to defending liberal values, preferring instead utopian visions of politics that can neither be tested nor implemented. For much of the twentieth century, as Hollander (2016) explains, the illiberalism of intellectuals was evident in the hero worship of dictators in places like Germany, China, Cuba, the Soviet Union, Cambodia, and Venezuela. Western intellectuals looked to strongmen on both the left and the right as figures of inspiration because of a "painful awareness of the inability of Western, pluralistic, capitalist societies to deliver sustaining values and beliefs that would enable them to confront and weather the endemic crises and frustrations of life, and especially modern life" (ibid., 294).

These same frustrations not only led Western intellectuals to admire dictators; they also brought them to nihilistic positions against Enlightenment traditions like liberalism. The identification with authoritarian figures and the rejection of "Western liberalism" are impulses of what Pascal Bruckner (2010, 21) calls a masochistic "penitential class," who, because of their guilt about colonialism, turn their back on the values of the Enlightenment. Today, radical scholars from the Global North seek to theorize the Global South in opposition to a static, liberal North/West. Some are so cavalier that they dismiss even the most humane of Enlightenment traditions such as human rights. For example, Jean and John Comaroff (2001, 39–40), purveyors of "theory from the south," diminish the value of human rights by comparing rights-based thinking to contemporary capitalism, contending that "If law underpins the langue of neoliberalism, constitutionalism has become the parole of universal human rights, a global argot that individuates the citizen and, by making cultural identity a private asset, rather than a collective claim, transmutes difference into likeness."

Such purple prose is merely academese for the tired argument that individualistic human rights are incompatible with collectivist societies. In fact, the same argument was better phrased by the spokesperson of the authoritarian Philippine president Rodrigo Duterte, when he was justifying the murder of thousands of drug suspects. "The liberal Western values being imposed upon an Asian nation that places premium on common good," he argued, "is both insensitive and displays a lack of appreciation for the diversity of global culture" (Quoted in Esmaquel 2017). Western intellectuals do not always directly endorse demagogues, but they are tempted by cool detachment to speak like them.

Hollander (2016, 9) contends that many pro-dictatorship intellectuals endorsed authoritarianism from a distance, and many of them "had little to gain, or lose" in their judgments. Until today, many illiberal commentators on the Global South from the Global North do so from far away, secure that constitutional rights do not collapse overnight in places like the United States or Europe—Donald Trump and the European far-right notwithstanding. Unfortunately, for those of us in places like the Philippines, a human rights regime may disintegrate overnight, as in the case of Duterte's Philippines. Rizal's country was once a broken, if relatively stable, liberal democracy. After the collapse of Ferdinand Marcos's dictatorship in 1986, it slowly inched its way toward some semblance of a liberal democracy, where regular elections occurred, civil society movements focused on institution building, and relatively open elections occurred (Quimpo 2008; Curato 2015; Thompson 1996). In 2016, the country was taken over by a murderous demagogue.

This collapse of liberal democracy occurs amid thunderous applause, with Duterte remaining popular despite a drug war that has killed thousands. Because Duterte has devalued his country's human rights tradition—"If it concern human rights, I don't give a shit"—he once claimed (Quoted in Holmes 2016)—he has also devalued life. Survey data shows that the majority of Filipinos believe that extra-judicial killings are occurring under the drug war, yet a significant majority remain supportive of the government's draconian campaign (Pulse Asia Research Inc. 2017). Such is the moral crisis that Duterte has created.

When Rizal argued that pain purified liberalism, he was expressing a profound but obvious insight: Those who have had liberty denied them value it even more. Those who believe that liberty may slip away are more cautious in their criticisms of basic freedoms. For a liberal in the Philippines, the truth of this message can be found in the most quotidian contexts. Many liberals in my country have had to fight for liberal values in religious schools, patriarchal families, and other conservative institutions. Under Duterte, they fight amid an electorate that is increasingly proving susceptible to the temptations of authoritarianism. It is an everyday struggle for everyday changes.

Liberalism continues to be pragmatic. It is pragmatic for those who see the concrete needs of postcolonies, for thinkers like Rizal who seek evolving modernities for their nations. For Nigerian philosopher Olúfẹ́mi Táíwò (2014, 10), seeking these modernities requires being less concerned with the provenance of ideas and more with their usefulness. He contends "that the countries of Asia and Latin America that have transformed themselves for the better are precisely the ones that have wised up to the idea that—regardless of what they think of modernity and the West, which has most benefited from its proliferation—a good way to improve their lot in the world is to borrow some pages from the West's playbook."

While liberalism is an inadequate philosophy—it constantly has to grapple with its bourgeois origins—many of its principles are necessary checks against the excesses of political power. The fault of liberalism's critics has been to view it as an ends in itself instead of a system of guarantees, a bare minimum of treating citizens in a political community with what Orwell called "common decency." The history of liberalism has shown how many ideas can be grafted onto the liberal project. Social democracy, for example, represented liberalism coming to terms with class inequality. And, indeed, as Tony Judt (2010, 52) has argued, it was the welfare that bound citizens to the state's liberal institutions.

Liberalism grows. Liberal America once had slaves. Liberal countries from across the world refused women the right to vote. And many liberal states once had colonies, which they exploited. But because of anti-colonial liberals like Rizal, we now recognize colonialism as a contradiction of the liberal project. This recognition is a gift of the Enlightenment, and someone like Rizal had no qualms about appropriating what he saw in Europe, and grafting them into colonial contexts. He would have agreed with Bruckner (2010, 28) who contends that "There is no doubt that Europe has given birth to monsters, but at the same time it has given birth to theories that make it possible to understand and destroy these monsters."

The rise of global populism and authoritarianism means we can no longer dismiss liberal principles as lightly, since anti-liberalism feeds into the rhetoric of present-day dictators. The Philippine liberal tradition runs deep, but it is always in a precarious position, especially now. For those of us who seek comfort amid the tribulations of the present, we may return to Rizal's enigmatic vision of liberalism being a "plant that never dies." The liberal tradition may be in tatters, but we only need to replant its seeds and await its resurrection.

Bibliography

Bruckner, Pascal. 2010. *The Tyranny of Guilt: An Essay on Western Masochism.* Trans. Steven Rendall. Princeton: Princeton University Press.

Claudio, Lisandro E. 2017. Defending Liberalism in the Global South: Notes from Duterte's Philippines. *The Global South* 11 (2): 92–107.

Comaroff, Jean, and John L. Comaroff. 2001. Millenial Capitalism: First Thoughts on a Second Coming. In *Millennial Capitalism and the Culture of Neoliberalism,* ed. Jean Comaroff and John L. Comaroff, 1–56. Durham: Duke University Press.

Curato, Nicole. 2015. Deliberative Capacity as an Indicator of Democratic Quality: The Case of the Philippines. *International Political Science Review* 36 (1): 99–116.

Furet, Francois. 2000. *The Passing of an Illusion: The Idea of Communism in the Twentieth Century.* Trans. Deborah Furet. Chicago/London: University of Chicago Press.

Go, Julian. 2017. Myths of Nation and Empire: The Logic of America's Liberal Empire-State. *Thesis 11* 139 (1): 69–83.

Hollander, Paul. 2016. *From Benito Mussolini to Hugo Chavez: Intellectuals and a Century of Political Hero Worship.* Cambridge: Cambridge University Press.

Holmes, Oliver. 2016. Duterte Says Children Killed in Philippines Drug War Are 'Collateral Damage.' *The Guardian*, October 17. https://www.theguardian. com/world/2016/oct/17/duterte-says-children-killed-in-philippines-drug-war-are-collateral-damage

Judt, Tony. 2010. *Ill Fares the Land.* New York: Penguin Press.

Mehta, Uday Singh. 1999. *Liberalism and Empire.* Chicago/London: University of Chicago Press.

Pulse Asia Research Inc. 2017. September 2017 Nationwide Survey on the Campaign Against Illegal Drugs. http://www.pulseasia.ph/september-2017-nationwide-survey-on-the-campaign-against-illegal-drugs/

Quimpo, Nathan Gilbert. 2008. *Contested Democracy and the Left in the Philippines After Marcos.* Governance and Political Change. Quezon City: Ateneo de Manila University Press.

Táíwò, Olúfẹ́mi. 2014. *Africa Must Be Modern: A Manifesto.* Bloomington/ Indianapolis: Indiana University Press.

Thompson, Mark R. 1996. Off the Endangered List: Philippine Democratization in Comparative Perspective. *Comparative Politics* 28 (2): 179–205.

SHORTHAND CITATIONS FOR RIZAL'S WORKS

Fili—*El Filibusterismo*. Translated by Harold Augenbraum. New York: Penguin Books, 2011.

Letters to Blumentritt—*Jose Rizal Correspondence with Blumentritt*. 2011. Manila: National Historical Commission of the Philippines.

Misc. Letters—*Jose Rizal Miscellaneous Correspondences*. 2011: Manila: National Historical Commission of the Philippines.

Noli—*Noli Me Tangere*. Translated by Harold Augenbraum. New York: Penguin Books, 2006.

PHW—*Jose Rizal Political and Historical Writings*. 2011. Manila: National Historical Commission of the Philippines.

Reformists—*Jose Rizal Correspondence with Fellow Reformists*. 2011. Manila: National Historical Commission of the Philippines.

© The Author(s) 2019
L. E. Claudio, *Jose Rizal*, Global Political Thinkers,
https://doi.org/10.1007/978-3-030-01316-5

BIBLIOGRAPHY

Abinales, Patricio N., and Donna J. Amoroso. 2017. *State and Society in the Philippines.* 2nd ed. Quezon City: Ateneo de Manila University Press.

Agoncillo, Teodoro A. 1956. *The Revolt of the Masses.* Quezon City: University of the Philippines.

Aguilar, Filomeno V. 2005. Tracing Origins: Ilustrado Nationalism and the Racial Science of Migration Waves. *The Journal of Asian Studies* 64 (03): 605–637.

———. 2011. Filibustero, Rizal, and the Manilamen of the Nineteenth Century. *Philippine Studies* 59 (4): 429–469.

Anderson, Benedict R.O'G. 1983. *Imagined Communities: Reflections on the Origin and Spread of Nationalism.* London/New York: Verso.

———. 1998. *The Spectre of Comparisons: Nationalism, Southeast Asia, and the World.* New York: Verso.

———. 2007. *Under Three Flags: Anarchism and the Anti-Colonial Imagination.* Pasig City: Anvil Publishing Inc.

Bernad, Miguel A. 1986. *Rizal and Spain: An Essay in Biographical Context.* Metro Manila: National Book Store.

Blumentritt, Ferdinand. 1891. Sketches. *La Solidaridad* Year 3, no. 49. In *La Solidaridad*, vol. 3, Trans. Guadalupe Fores-Ganzon. Pasig City: Fundacion Santiago, 1996.

Bruckner, Pascal. 2010. *The Tyranny of Guilt: An Essay on Western Masochism.* Trans. Steven Rendall. Princeton: Princeton University Press.

Carr, Raymond. 1966. *Spain, 1808–1939.* Oxford: Clarendon Press.

© The Author(s) 2019
L. E. Claudio, *Jose Rizal,* Global Political Thinkers,
https://doi.org/10.1007/978-3-030-01316-5

Castroverde, Aaron C. 2013. *Jose Rizal and the Spanish Novel*. PhD Dissertation, Duke University.

Chibber, Vivek. 2014. Making Sense of Postcolonial Theory: A Response to Gayatri Chakravorty Spivak. *Cambridge Review of International Affairs* 27 (3): 617–624.

Claudio, Lisandro E. 2013. Postcolonial Fissures and the Contingent Nation An Antinationalist Critique of Philippine Historiography. *Philippine Studies: Historical and Ethnographic Viewpoints* 61 (1): 45–75.

———. 2017. *Liberalism and the Postcolony: Thinking the State in 20th-Century Philippines*. Singapore: NUS Press.

———. 2017. Defending Liberalism in the Global South: Notes from Duterte's Philippines. *The Global South* 11 (2): 92–107.

Coates, Austin. 1992. *Rizal, Philippine Nationalist and Martyr*. Manila: Solidaridad Publishing House.

Comaroff, Jean, and John L. Comaroff. 2001. Millenial Capitalism: First Thoughts on a Second Coming. In *Millennial Capitalism and the Culture of Neoliberalism*, ed. Jean Comaroff and John L. Comaroff, 1–56. Durham: Duke University Press.

Constantino, Renato. 2005. Veneration Without Understanding. *The Philippine Reporter*, June 16. http://philippinereporter.com/2005/06/16/veneration-without-understanding/

Corpuz, O.D. 1989. *The Roots of the Filipino Nation, Volume II*. Quezon City: Aklahi Foundation, Inc.

Curato, Nicole. 2015. Deliberative Capacity as an Indicator of Democratic Quality: The Case of the Philippines. *International Political Science Review* 36 (1): 99–116.

Daroy, Petronilo Bn. 1968. Crisostomo Ibarra. In *Rizal: Contrary Essays*, ed. Petronilo Bn. Daroy and Dolores S. Feria. Quezon City: Guro Books.

De Llobet, Ruth. 2009. El Poeta, El Regidor y La Amante: Manila y La Emergencia de Una Identidad Criolla Filipina. *Istor: Revista de Historia Internacional* 38: 65–92.

Esmaquel II, Paterno. 2016. PH Rejects 'Interference' of UN in 'Household Affairs.' *Rappler*, August 20. https://www.rappler.com/nation/143661-philippines-united-nations-investigation-drug-killings

Evans, Richard J. 2016. *The Pursuit of Power*. New York: Viking.

Furet, Francois. 2000. *The Passing of an Illusion: The Idea of Communism in the Twentieth Century*. Trans. Deborah Furet. Chicago/London: University of Chicago Press.

Go, Julian. 2017. Myths of Nation and Empire: The Logic of America's Liberal Empire-State. *Thesis 11* 139 (1): 69–83.

Gray, John. 2000. *Two Faces of Liberalism*. New York: The New Press.

Guerrero, Leon Ma. 2012. *The First Filipino: A Biography of Jose Rizal*. Makati City: Guerrero Publishing.

————. 2013. Rizal as Liberal; Bonifacio and Democrat. In *Pens as Swords: The Philippine PEN Jose Rizal Lectures, 1958–2007*, ed. Jose Victor Torres. Manila: Solidaridad Publishing House.

Guillermo, Ramon. 2017. Andres Bonifacio: Proletarian Hero of the Philippines and Indonesia. *Inter-Asia Cultural Studies* 18 (3): 338–346.

Hau, Caroline S. 2000. *Necessary Fictions: Philippine Literature and the Nation, 1946–1980.* Quezon City: Ateneo de Manila University Press.

————. 2004. *On the Subject of the Nation: Filipino Writings from the Margins, 1981–2004.* Quezon City: Ateneo de Manila University Press.

————. 2017a. *Elites and Ilustrados in Philippine Culture.* Quezon City: Ateneo de Manila University Press.

————. 2017b. Did Padre Damaso Rape Pia Alba?: Reticence, Revelation, and Revolution in Jose Rizal's Novels. *Philippine Studies: Historical and Ethnographic Viewpoints* 65 (2): 137–199.

Hobsbawm, Eric J. 1989. *The Age of Empire, 1875–1914.* New York: Vintage Books.

————. 1996. *The Age of Revolution: 1789–1848.* New York: Vintage.

————. 1997. *The Age of Capital, 1848–1875.* London: Abacus.

Hollander, Paul. 2016. *From Benito Mussolini to Hugo Chavez: Intellectuals and a Century of Political Hero Worship.* Cambridge: Cambridge University Press.

Holmes, Oliver. 2016. Duterte Says Children Killed in Philippines Drug War Are 'Collateral Damage.' *The Guardian*, October 17. https://www.theguardian.com/world/2016/oct/17/duterte-says-children-killed-in-philippines-drug-war-are-collateral-damage

Joaquin, Nick. 2005. *A Question of Heroes.* Pasig City: Anvil Publishing Inc.

Judt, Tony. 2010. *Ill Fares the Land.* New York: Penguin Press.

Kirsch, Adam. 2016. Melancholy Liberalism. *City Journal*, Winter. http://www.city-journal.org/2016/26_1_melancholy-liberalism.html

Legarda, Benito. 2011. The Economic Background of Rizal's Time. *The Philippine Review of Economics* XLVIII (2): 1–22.

Mead, Walter Russell. 2013. A Historical Look at American Liberalism. Interview by Charles R. Kesler. Youtube Video, September 12. https://www.youtube.com/watch?v=pRCTg5OWlZs

Mehta, Uday Singh. 1999. *Liberalism and Empire.* Chicago/London: University of Chicago Press.

Mojares, Resil B. 1983. *Origins and Rise of the Filipino Novel: A Generic Study of the Novel Until 1940.* Quezon City: University of the Philippines Press.

————. 2006. *Brains of the Nation: Pedro Paterno, T.H. Pardo de Tavera, Isabelo de Los Reyes and the Production of Modern Knowledge.* Quezon City: Ateneo de Manila University Press.

————. 2013. *Isabelo's Archive.* Manila: Anvil Publishing Inc.

————. 2017. *Interrogations in Philippine Cultural History: The Ateneo de Manila Lectures.* Quezon City: Ateneo de Manila University Press.

Ocampo, Ambeth. 1992. *Makamisa: The Search for Rizal's Third Novel.* Pasig: Anvil Publishing Inc.

———. 2012. *Rizal Without the Overcoat.* Pasig City: Anvil Publishing Inc.

———. 2013. *Meaning and History: The Rizal Lectures.* Revised ed. Pasig City: Anvil Publishing Inc.

Palma, Rafael. 1949. *Biografia de Rizal.* Manila: Bureau of Print.

Perry, Martin, et al. 2009. *Western Civilization: Ideas, Politics, and Society.* 9th ed. Boston/New York: Houghton Mifflin Harcourt Publishing Company.

Polasky, Janet. 2015. *Revolutions Without Borders: The Call to Liberty in the Atlantic World.* New Haven: Yale University Press.

Pulse Asia Research Inc. 2017. September 2017 Nationwide Survey on the Campaign Against Illegal Drugs. http://www.pulseasia.ph/september-2017-nationwide-survey-on-the-campaign-against-illegal-drugs/

Quibuyen, Floro. 1997. Rizal and the Revolution. *Philippine Studies: Historical and Ethnographic Viewpoints* 45 (2): 225–257.

Quimpo, Nathan Gilbert. 2008. *Contested Democracy and the Left in the Philippines After Marcos.* Governance and Political Change. Quezon City: Ateneo de Manila University Press.

Rafael, Vicente L. 2015. Introduction: Revolutionary Contradictions. In *Luzon at War: Contradictions in Philippine Society, 1898–1902,* ed. Milagros Camayon Guerrero, 1–19. Mandaluyong City: Anvil Publishing Inc.

Retana, Wenceslao. 1907. *Vida y Escritos Del Dr. Jose Rizal.* Madrid: Liberaria General de V. Suarez.

Ryan, Alan. 2012. *The Making of Modern Liberalism.* Princeton/Oxford: Princeton University Press.

Sarkisyanz, Manuel. 1995. *Rizal and Republican Spain and Other Rizalist Essays.* Manila: National Historical Institute.

Schumacher, John N. 1991. *The Making of a Nation: Essays on Nineteenth-Century Filipino Nationalism.* Quezon City: Ateneo de Manila University Press.

———. 1997. *The Propaganda Movement: 1880–1895: The Creation of a Filipino Consciousness, the Making of a Revolution.* Quezon City: Ateneo de Manila University Press.

Sison, Jose Maria. 1966. Rizal the Social Critic, December 29. https://josemaria-sison.org/rizal-the-social-critic/

Táíwò, Olúfẹ́mi. 2014. *Africa Must Be Modern: A Manifesto.* Bloomington/Indianapolis: Indiana University Press.

Thomas, Megan C. 2012. *Orientalists, Propagandists, and Ilustrados: Filipino Scholarship and the End of Spanish Colonialism.* Minneapolis/London: University of Minnesota Press.

Thompson, Mark R. 1996. Off the Endangered List: Philippine Democratization in Comparative Perspective. *Comparative Politics* 28 (2): 179–205.

Zinoman, Peter. 2013. *Vietnamese Colonial Republican: The Political Vision of Vũ Trọng Phụng.* Berkeley: University of California Press.

Index[1]

NUMBERS AND SYMBOLS

1868 Glorious Revolution, 7
1872, 11, 56, 64

A

Agoncillo, Teodoro A., 32
Aguilar, Filomeno, 15n3, 56n1
Alejandrino, Jose, 46, 49
American Declaration of
    independence, ix
American Revolution, vii, 2, 31
American revolutionaries, 31
Anarchism, xi
Anderson, Benedict R. O'G., viii, 3,
    40, 63, 66
Ateneo Municipal, 14
Augenbaum, Harold, xiii

B

Balzac, Honore de, 39n1
Barcelona, 12, 14

Barrantes, Vicente, 46
Basa, Jose Ma., 39n1
Basilio, 58, 59, 62
Bayot Conspiracy, 6
Bayot Mutiny, 7
Benthan, Jeremy, 72
Beranger, Pierre Jean de, 39n1
Berlin, 15
Bismarck, Otto von, 26
Blumentritt, Ferdinand, 15, 16, 18,
    25, 56, 57, 65
Bolshevik Revolution, 2
Bonaparte, Joseph, 4
Bonifacio, Andres, 18
Bracken, Josephine, 17
British North Borneo, 17
Bruckner, Pascal, 76
Brussels, 15
Buencamino, Felipe, 9
Bulacan, 9
Burg, Father, 48
Burgos, Fr. Jose, 10, 11, 14, 17, 19,
    29, 48, 56, 59

[1] Note: Page numbers followed by 'n' refer to notes.

© The Author(s) 2019   85
L. E. Claudio, *Jose Rizal*, Global Political Thinkers,
https://doi.org/10.1007/978-3-030-01316-5

C
Cabesang Tales, 59
Cadiz Constitution, 4, 5, 19
Calamba, 13, 15, 16, 43, 59
Carlist wars, 6
Carlos V., 6
Carr, Raymond, 4, 5
Castroverde, Aaron C., 38
Cavite, 9, 11, 18
Chekov, Anton, 13
Chibber, Vivek, x
Civic liberalism, 25
Civil Guard, 50–52
Civil liberties, 25, 51, 58
Coates, Austin, 17
Comaroff, Jean, 74
Comaroff, John, 74
Comite de Reformadores, 9, 10, 13
Communism, 73
Communist Party of the Philippines, x
Communists, xi
Concert of Europe, 2
Conrad, Joseph, 13
Constantino, Renato, 66
Constitution of Cadiz, 23
Corpuz, O.D., 9
Cortes, 4, 9
Creoles, 3, 4, 11, 13, 19, 48, 49, 59, 67, 73
Creolism, 44
Crisis of '72, 11
Crispin, 58
Cristina, Maria, 6
Cuban Revolution, 18
Custodio, Don, 24, 60, 61

D
Damaso, Father, 44, 45
Dapitan, 17
Daroy, Petronilo Bn., 46, 52
Daudet, Alphonse, 39

de La Torre, Carlos Maria, 28
de Labra, Rafael Maria, 12
de los Reyes, Ventura, 5
de Morga, Antonio, 15
de Taveras, Pardo, 6
Declaration of the Rights of Man, ix
del Pilar, Marcelo H., 16, 65
dela Cruz, Apolonario, 7
Dickens, Charles, 39
Dominican, 15
Don Santiago de los Santos, 44
Dumas, Alexander, ix, 39n1
Duterte, Rodrigo, xii, 74, 75

E
El Filibusterismo, 15, 16, 24, 64
"El Triunfo de la Muerte Sobre la Vida," 24
Elias, 45–47, 49–52, 58, 66
End of history, 73
Enlightenment, ix, 23–25, 27, 39, 73, 74, 76
Evans, Richard J., 22
The execution of Burgos, Gomez, and Zamora in 1872, 43
Execution of the secular priests in 1872, 14

F
Fascism, 73
Feminism, 34
Ferdinand VII, 5, 6
Fili, 57–61, 63, 66, 67, 69
Filibusterism, 56
Filibusterismo, xiii, 56
Filibusteros, 55, 56, 60, 62, 66
Filipino liberals, 28, 48, 49
Filipinos, 10, 67
First Carlist War, 9
Florentino, Fr., 62–66

Freethinker, 12
French Declaration of the Rights of
     Man, 16, 26
French Revolution, vii, 2, 4, 19, 23
Freud, Sigmund, 13
Friar control, 7
Friars, 27, 30, 42, 52, 53, 59
Furet, Francois, 73

G
Gandhi, Mohandas, 13
Girondins, 2
Global North, 74
Global South, xi, 71, 72, 74
Go, Julian, 72
Gomes, Mariano, 11
Gomez, Fr., 56
Gray, John, 24
Guerrero, Leon Ma, 25, 31, 32

H
Hau, Caroline S., 12, 37, 40, 41n4,
     42, 43n5, 44, 46, 49, 60n4, 68
Heidelberg, 15
Hidalgo, Felix Resurrection, 39
Ho Chi Minh, 30
Hobsbawm, Eric J., 22
Hollander, Paul, 74
Hong Kong, 16, 26, 29
Hugo, Victor, ix, 27, 39
Human rights, 74

I
Ibarra, Juan Crisostomo, 43–50, 52,
     55, 56, 58, 63
Illiberal democracy, 73
Illiberalism, xii
Ilustrados, xi, 11, 12, 19, 40
Inquilinos, 13, 15

Inquisition, 64
Isabella II, 9
Isagani, 62

J
Jacobins, 2, 65
Jefferson, Thomas, 3
Jesuits, 14, 25
Joaquin, Nick, 4, 5, 8, 11, 48, 64

K
Katipunan, 1, 18, 26

L
La Juventud Escolar Liberal, 9, 13, 14
La Liga Filipina, 17–19, 32
La Solidaridad, 12, 16, 28, 53, 63,
     65, 66
La Torre, Carlos Maria de, 9, 11, 43
Laguna, 8, 13
Larra, Mariano de, 27
Latin American revolutions of
     1808–1825, 3
La última razón, 69
Legarda, Benito, 6
Lenin, 13, 14
Liberal democracy, 73
Liberalism, vii, xi, 2, 19, 21–24, 26,
     28, 33, 38, 52, 69, 72
     for the colonized, 27
     for the colony, 23, 52
     in the colony, 23
     in Rizal's Philippines, 24
Liberal reform, 69
Liberal reformism, 43
Liberal republic, 68
Liberal revolt, 65
Liberal revolution, 31, 64
Liberal Rizal, 26

Liberal Spaniards, 61
Liga, 17
Lopez Jaena, Graciano, 63, 64, 66
Lopez, Leoncio, 65
Louis XIV, 64
Louis XV, 64
Luna, Juan, 38, 39

M
Macaulay, Lord, 72
Madrid, 14
Manila, 8, 13, 14, 18
Marcos, Ferdinand, 49n10, 75
Maria Clara, 43–47
Masonic, ix, 19
Masonry, 13
Masons, 13, 17
Mazzini, Giuseppe, 3, 26
Mead, Walter Russel, xi
Mehta, Uday Singh, 23, 72
Mendizabal, Jose Alvarez, 6
Mercado, Paciano, 9, 14
Mercados, 13, 15
Metternich system, 2
Mill, James, 72
Mill, J.S., 23, 72
Mi Ultimo Adios, 33
Modus vivendi, 24
Mojares, Resil B., 3, 40
Moliere, 39n1
Monjuich, 18
Montesquieu, Charles de Secondat,
    39n1
Morayta, Miguel, 12

N
Napoleon Bonaparte, 2
Nationalism, 2
Nazis, xi
Nehru, ix

Ninay, 40n2
Noli me Tangere, xiii, 15, 34, 39–43,
    43n5, 46, 48, 49, 52, 53, 55, 57,
    58
North Americans, 67
Novales, Andres, 6
Novales Revolt, 6, 7
Novels, 38

O
Ocampo, Ambeth, xii
Orwell, George, xi, 76

P
Paciano, 16
Paine, 6
Palma, Rafael, 46, 49
Paris, 15
Parnaso Filipino, 5
Paterno, Pedro, 40n2
Penguin Classics, viii
Philippine liberalism, 2, 10, 13
Philippine Revolution of 1896, vii, xii,
    2, 32
Philippines, 40, 42–44, 52, 58, 68,
    74
Pi Y Margall, Francisco, 12
Piddington, Henry, 6
Polasky, Janet, 22
Ponce, Mariano, 11, 13, 28, 48, 53,
    64, 67
Posada, Vicente, 5
Postcolonial theory, 71
Proudhonian, 52
Pule, Hermano, 7

Q
Quibuyen, Floro, 32, 67
Quiroga, 59

R
Reactionary, 53
Regidors, 6
Republicanism, 13
Retana, Wenceslao, 42
Revolutions in Spain's American
    colonies, 41
Riego, Rafael de, 5
River Pasig, 45
Rizal, Jose, vii–x, xii, xiii, 1, 7, 11, 13,
    14, 16, 17, 19, 21, 23–27, 29,
    32, 38, 41n3, 42, 46, 46n8, 49,
    52, 64, 65, 67, 72, 75, 76
Rizal's annotation of Morga's work,
    15n3
Rizal's novels, 38, 41
Rizal's radicalism, 38
Rousseau, Jean-Jacques, 6
Russian and Chinese revolutions, 30
Ryan, Alan, xi

S
Salazar, Pedro Antonio (Governor
    General), 7
Salvi, Father, 45, 62
San Diego, 43, 44, 58, 59
Schiller, Friedrich, 42
Schumacher, John N., 9, 13, 14, 27, 45
"Secularization" of parishes, 10
Simoun, 58, 62–65
Simoun wind, 59
Sisa, 58
Sison, Jose Maria, x
Spain's liberal Cadiz Constitution, ix
Spanish friars, 27
Spanish Glorious Revolution of 1868,
    43
Spanish liberalism, 38, 52
Spanish liberals, 27, 28, 61, 72
Spoliarium, 38
Sucesos de las Islas Filipinas, 15
Sue, Eugene, 39

Suez, 43
Sun Yat-Sen, ix, 13

T
Tagalog, 41, 47
Tagore, 13
Táíwò, Olúfẹmi, 75
Tasio the Philosopher, 47, 52
Thomas, Megan C., 10, 23
Tiago, Captain, 44, 45
Tinchang, Captain, 48
Tinong, Captain, 48
Tobacco monopoly, 8
Tragedy of 1872, 48
Trienio Liberal, 5
Trump, Donald, 74

U
University of Santo Tomas, 9, 10, 14,
    42

V
Varela, Luis Rodriguez, 4, 5, 11, 19,
    44, 48
Voltaire, ix, 6
Volteriano (Volterian), 12
Vũ Trọng Phụng, ix

W
The Wandering Jew, 39
Weber, Max, 13
Weyler, Valeriano (Governor General),
    16, 59
"What Must Be Done" (Lenin), 30

Z
Zamora, Jacinto, 11, 56
Zola, Emile, 39, 39n1

CPSIA information can be obtained
at www.ICGtesting.com
Printed in the USA
LVHW010123061118
596007LV00013B/393/P